enVisionmath 2.0

Volume 2B Topics 12–15

Authors

Randall I. Charles
Professor Emeritus
Department of Mathematics
San Jose State University
San Jose, California

Jennifer Bay-Williams
Professor of Mathematics Education
College of Education and Human Development
University of Louisville
Louisville, Kentucky

Robert Q. Berry, III
Associate Professor of Mathematics Education
Department of Curriculum, Instruction and Special Education
University of Virginia
Charlottesville, Virginia

Janet H. Caldwell
Professor of Mathematics
Rowan University
Glassboro, New Jersey

Zachary Champagne
Assistant in Research
Florida Center for Research in Science, Technology, Engineering, and Mathematics (FCR-STEM)
Jacksonville, Florida

Juanita Copley
Professor Emerita, College of Education
University of Houston
Houston, Texas

Warren Crown
Professor Emeritus of Mathematics Education
Graduate School of Education
Rutgers University
New Brunswick, New Jersey

Francis (Skip) Fennell
L. Stanley Bowlsbey Professor of Education and Graduate and Professional Studies
McDaniel College
Westminster, Maryland

Karen Karp
Professor of Mathematics Education
Department of Early Childhood and Elementary Education
University of Louisville
Louisville, Kentucky

Stuart J. Murphy
Visual Learning Specialist
Boston, Massachusetts

Jane F. Schielack
Professor of Mathematics
Associate Dean for Assessment and Pre K–12 Education, College of Science
Texas A&M University
College Station, Texas

Jennifer M. Suh
Associate Professor for Mathematics Education
George Mason University
Fairfax, Virginia

Jonathan A. Wray
Mathematics Instructional Facilitator
Howard County Public Schools
Ellicott City, Maryland

SAVVAS
LEARNING COMPANY

Mathematicians

Roger Howe
Professor of Mathematics
Yale University
New Haven, Connecticut

Gary Lippman
Professor of Mathematics and
Computer Science
California State University, East Bay
Hayward, California

ELL Consultants

Janice R. Corona
Independent Education Consultant
Dallas, Texas

Jim Cummins
Professor
The University of Toronto
Toronto, Canada

Debbie Crisco
Math Coach
Beebe Public Schools
Beebe, Arkansas

Kathleen A. Cuff
Teacher
Kings Park Central School District
Kings Park, New York

Erika Doyle
Math and Science Coordinator
Richland School District
Richland, Washington

Reviewers

Susan Jarvis
Math and Science Curriculum Coordinator
Ocean Springs Schools
Ocean Springs, Mississippi

Copyright © 2017 by Savvas Learning Company LLC. All Rights Reserved. Printed in the United States of America.

This publication is protected by copyright, and permission should be obtained from the publisher prior to any prohibited reproduction, storage in a retrieval system, or transmission in any form or by any means, electronic, mechanical, photocopying, recording, or otherwise. For information regarding permissions, request forms, and the appropriate contacts within the Savvas Learning Company Rights Management group, please send your query to the address below.

Savvas Learning Company LLC, 15 East Midland Avenue, Paramus, NJ 07652

Savvas™ and **Savvas Learning Company™** are the exclusive trademarks of Savvas Learning Company LLC in the U.S. and other countries.

Savvas Learning Company publishes through its famous imprints **Prentice Hall®** and **Scott Foresman®** which are exclusive registered trademarks owned by Savvas Learning Company LLC in the U.S. and/or other countries.

enVisionMATH® and **Savvas Realize™** are exclusive trademarks of Savvas Learning Company LLC in the U.S. and/or other countries.

Unless otherwise indicated herein, any third party trademarks that may appear in this work are the property of their respective owners, and any references to third party trademarks, logos, or other trade dress are for demonstrative or descriptive purposes only. Such references are not intended to imply any sponsorship, endorsement, authorization, or promotion of Savvas Learning Company products by the owners of such marks, or any relationship between the owner and Savvas Learning Company LLC or its authors, licensees, or distributors.

ISBN-13: 978-0-328-93065-4
ISBN-10: 0-328-93065-2

TOPIC 12 Measure Lengths

Essential Question: What are ways to measure how long an object is?

Digital Resources

Solve Learn Glossary Tools Assessment Help Games

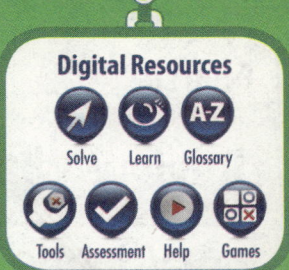

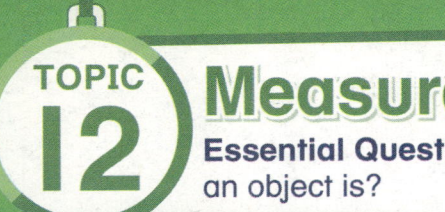

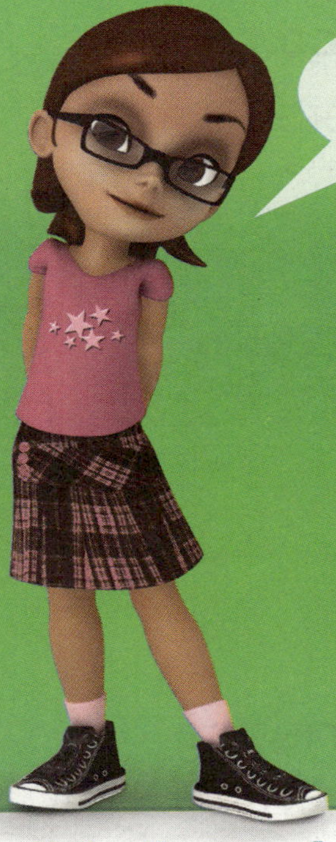

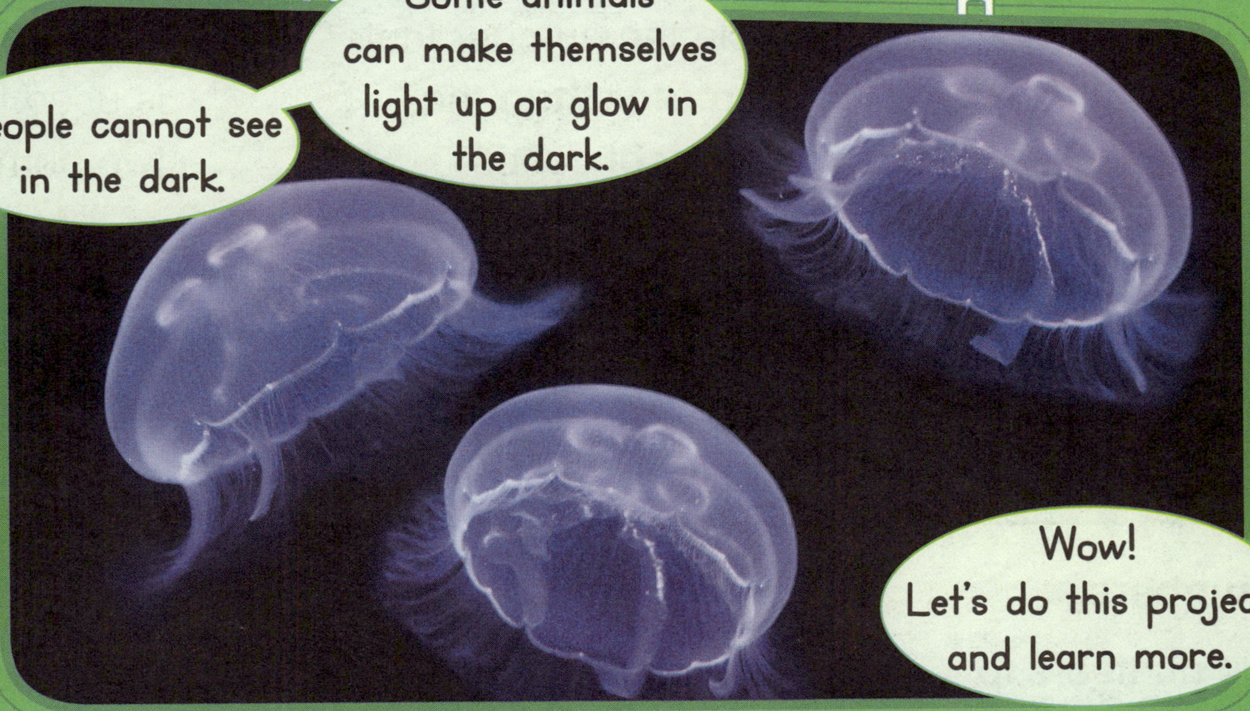

People cannot see in the dark.
Some animals can make themselves light up or glow in the dark.
Wow! Let's do this project and learn more.

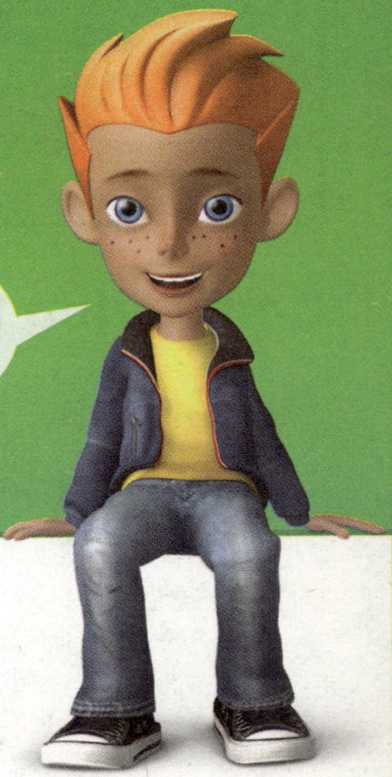

Math and Science Project: Now You See Me, Now You Don't!

Find Out Talk to friends and relatives about animals that can be seen in the dark. Ask how some animals can make themselves glow in the dark.

Journal: Make a Book Show what you found out. In your book, also:

- Draw pictures of animals that can glow in the dark.
- Think about how you could measure these animals.

Name _____

Review What You Know

Vocabulary

1. Circle the number that is **less than** the number of cubes.

   3   5   8

2. Circle the number that is **greater than** the number of cubes.

   1   3   5

3. Circle the symbol that is used to **compare** two numbers

   +   −   >

Comparing Numbers

4. Choose two numbers to make the sentence true.

   ____ is less than ____.

5. Charlie has 9 stickers. Pearl has 5 stickers. Write the numbers and the symbol to compare their numbers of stickers.

Counting

6. Write the missing numbers.

   6, 7, 8, ____, ____, 11, ____

662 six hundred sixty-two

My Word Cards

Study the words on the front of the card. Complete the activity on the back.

longest	shortest	longer
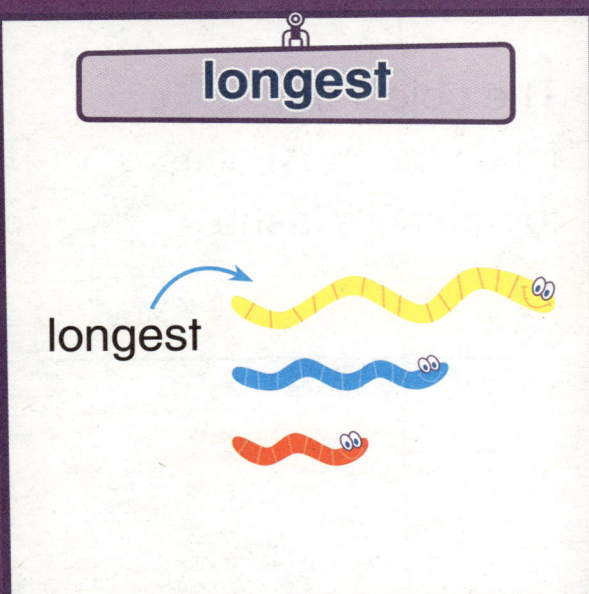		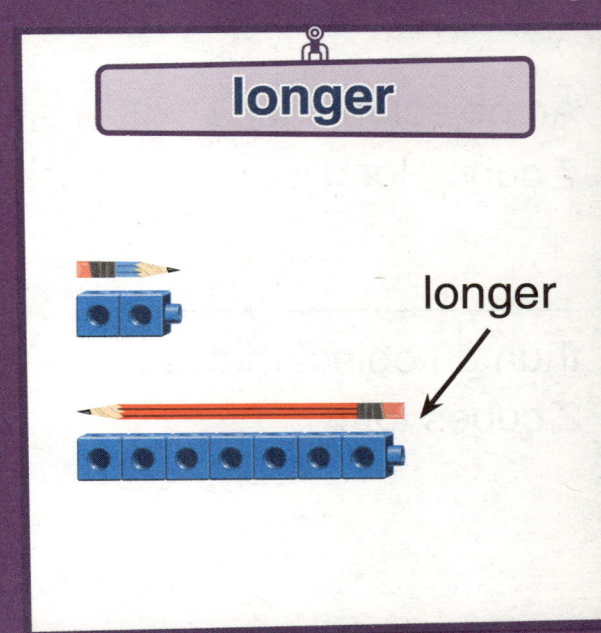
shorter	length	measure
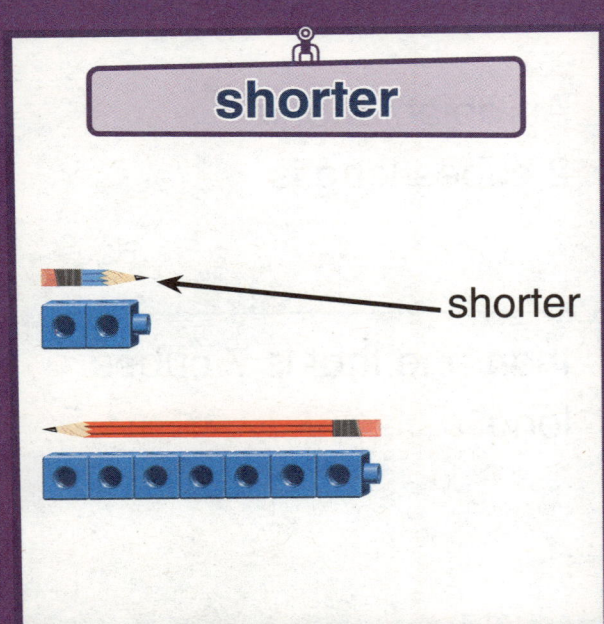	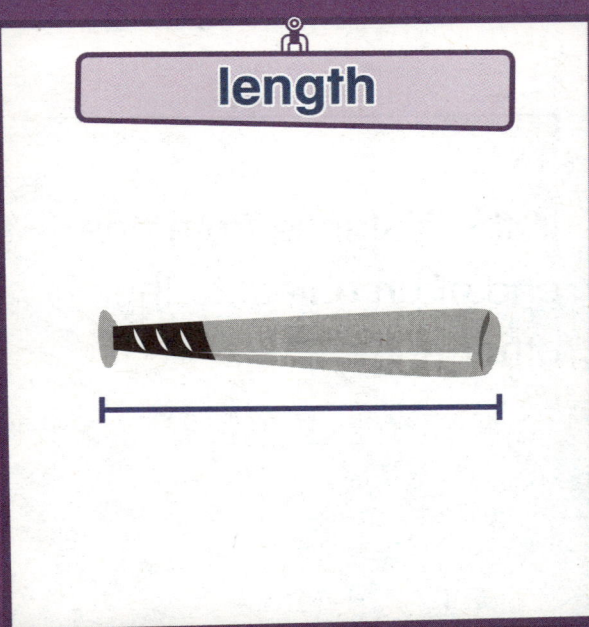	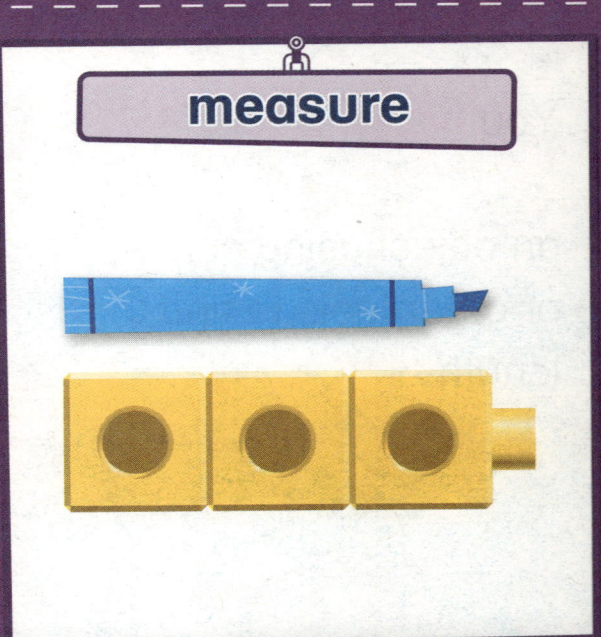

Topic 12 | My Word Cards

six hundred sixty-three **663**

My Word Cards

Use what you know to complete the sentences. Extend learning by writing your own sentence using each word.

An object that is 7 cubes long is _____ than an object that is 2 cubes long.	The _____ object is the one that takes the fewest units to measure.	The object that takes the most units to measure is the _____.
You _____ an object using cubes or other tools to find the length.	_____ is the distance from one end of an object to the other end.	An object that is 2 cubes long is _____ than one that is 7 cubes long.

664 six hundred sixty-four

My Word Cards

Study the words on the front of the card. Complete the activity on the back.

length unit

Topic 12 | My Word Cards

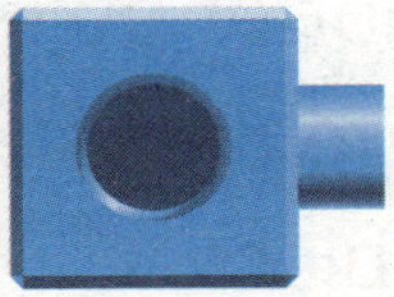

My Word Cards Use what you know to complete the sentence. Extend learning by writing your own sentence using each word.

A _____

_____ is the shorter object that you use to measure a longer object.

Name _____

Solve & Share

Can you put these objects in order from longest to shortest? How can you tell if one object is longer than another object?

Lesson 12-1
Compare and Order by Length

I can ...
order objects by length.

I can also be precise in my work.

Longest	
Shortest	

Topic 12 | Lesson 1 six hundred sixty-seven **667**

You can put the worms in order by **length**.

The yellow worm is **longer** than the red worm and the blue worm.

"The yellow worm is the longest."

The red worm is **shorter** than the blue worm.

longest

"The red worm is the shortest."

Now the worms are in order from longest to shortest.

longest

shortest

Do You Understand?

Show Me! Use the words "shorter" and "shortest" to describe two different worms above.

Guided Practice

Draw lines to show which object is longest and which is shortest.

1. longest ……………

   shortest ……………

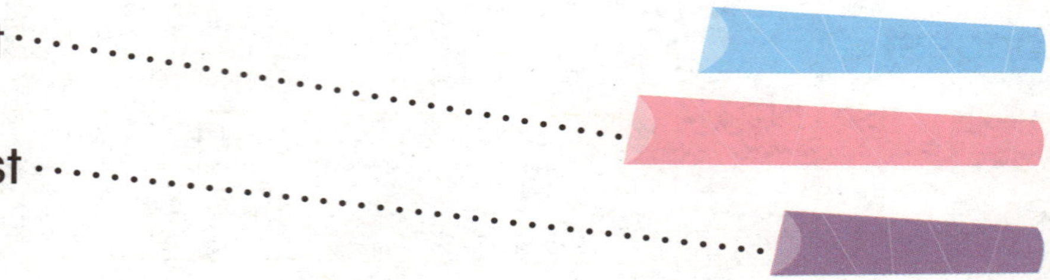

2. longest

   shortest

668 six hundred sixty-eight

Copyright © Savvas Learning Company LLC. All Rights Reserved.

Topic 12 | Lesson 1

Name _____

Independent Practice — Draw lines to show which object is longest and which is shortest.

3. longest

shortest

4. longest

shortest

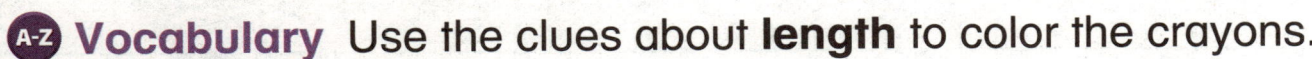 **Vocabulary** Use the clues about **length** to color the crayons.

5. The **shortest** crayon is orange.
The blue crayon is **longer** than the green crayon.

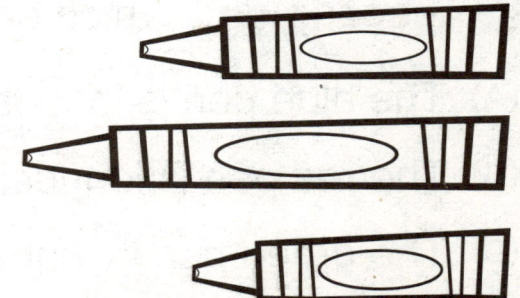

Topic 12 | Lesson 1 — six hundred sixty-nine **669**

Problem Solving Solve the problems below.

6. **Be Precise** Tomaz paints a line that is longer than the blue line. What color line did he paint? Use the pictures to solve. _____

7. **Be Precise** Amber's piece of chalk is shorter than the blue piece. What color is Amber's chalk? Use the pictures to solve. _____

8. **Higher Order Thinking** Draw 3 lines with different lengths in order from longest to shortest. Label the longest and shortest lines.

9. **Assessment** Which best describes the pens?

Ⓐ The blue pen is longest.
Ⓑ The red pen is longest.
Ⓒ The green pen is longest.
Ⓓ The blue pen is shortest.

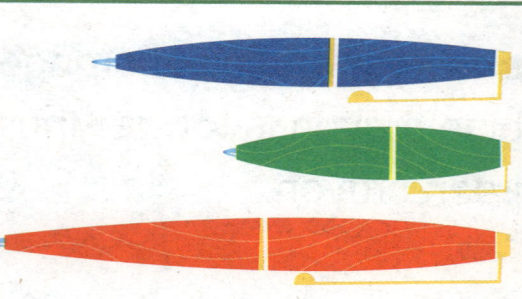

Name _____

Homework & Practice 12-1
Compare and Order by Length

Another Look! You can find the length of objects by comparing them.

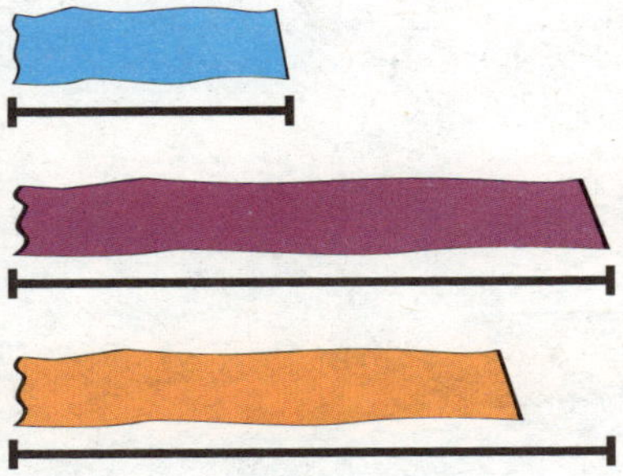

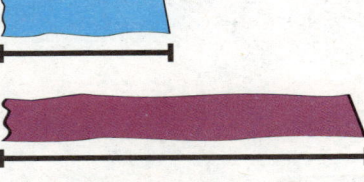

Which color of ribbon is the longest? _Purple_

Which color of ribbon is the shortest? _Blue_

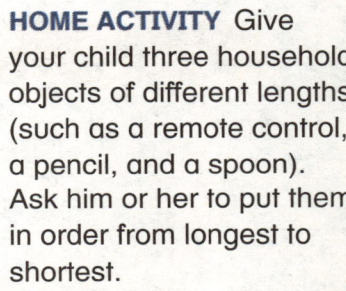

HOME ACTIVITY Give your child three household objects of different lengths (such as a remote control, a pencil, and a spoon). Ask him or her to put them in order from longest to shortest.

Write the number of the longest object.
Then write the number of the shortest object.

1. 1: ────────────────

2: ────────────────

3: ────────────────

Longest: ____   Shortest: ____

2.

Longest: ____   Shortest: ____

Topic 12 | Lesson 1   Digital Resources at SavvasRealize.com   six hundred seventy-one **671**

Circle the longest object. Cross out the shortest object.

3.

4.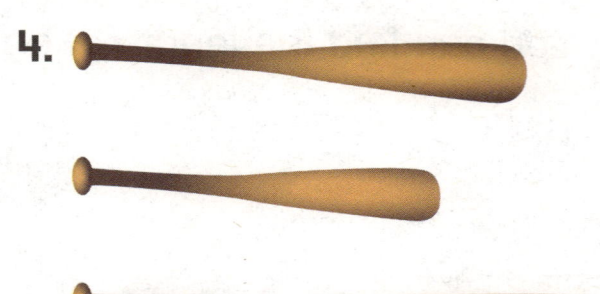

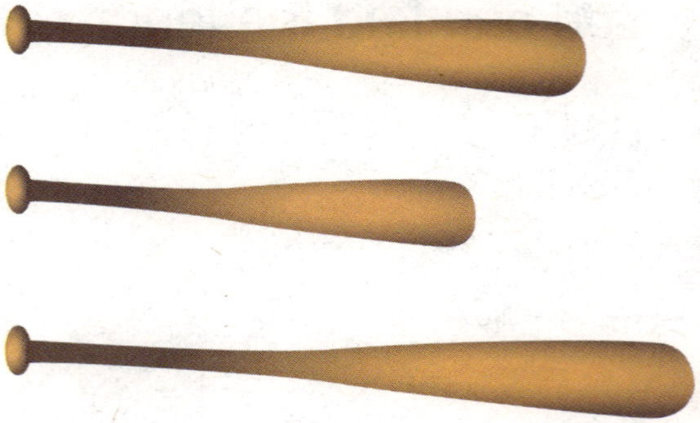

5. **Higher Order Thinking** Write the order of these 3 objects from longest to shortest:
Car   Bike   Airplane

_____

_____

6. **Assessment** Which book shown is the longest?

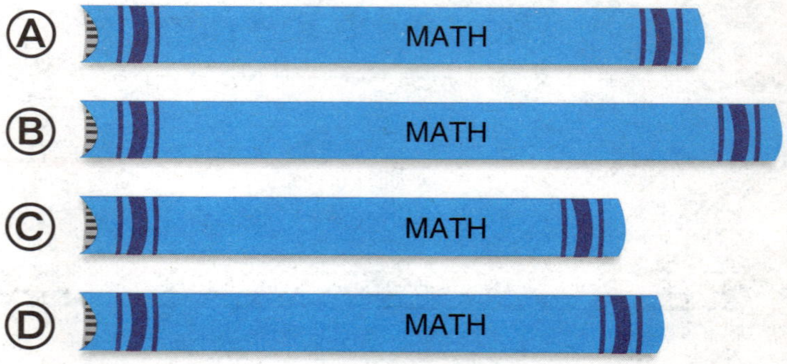

Ⓐ MATH
Ⓑ MATH
Ⓒ MATH
Ⓓ MATH

Name _____

Lesson 12-2
Indirect Measurement

Solve & Share

How can you find out whether the shoe or the pencil is longer without putting them next to each other? What can you use? Circle the longer object and explain how you found out.

I can ... indirectly compare objects by length.

I can also use math tools correctly.

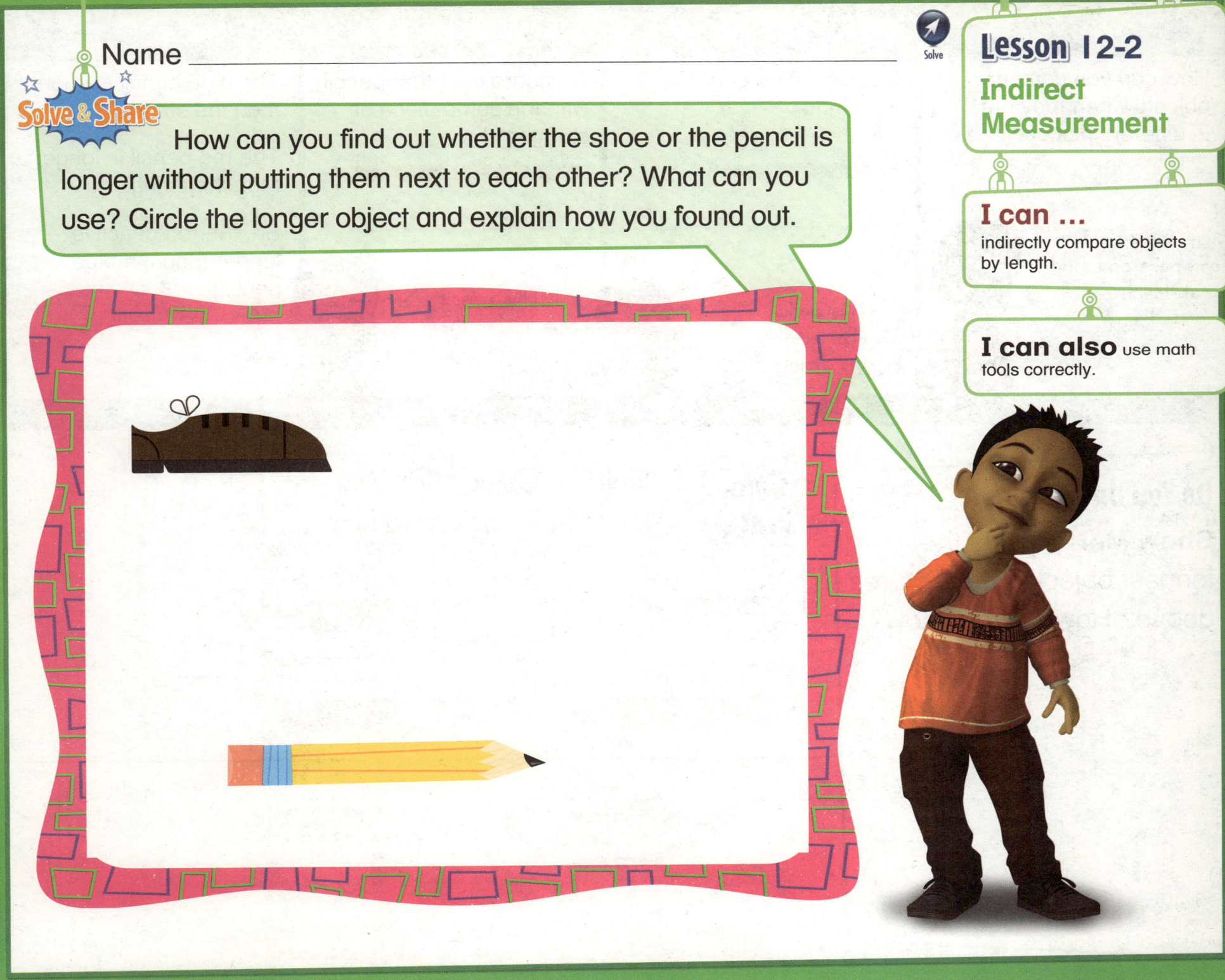

Topic 12 | Lesson 2 · Digital Resources at SavvasRealize.com · six hundred seventy-three **673**

How can you compare objects when they are in different places?

We can use one object to compare and find out which pencil is longer.

Compare one pencil with the string.

This pencil is shorter than the string.

Compare the other pencil with the same piece of string.

This pencil is longer than the string.

The blue pencil is shorter than the string.

The red pencil is longer than the string.

So, the red pencil is longer than the blue pencil.

Do You Understand?

Show Me! What is the longest object in the pictures above? How do you know?

☆ **Guided Practice** ☆ Circle the object that is longer. Use the **red** crayon to help.

1.

2.

674 six hundred seventy-four

Topic 12 | Lesson 2

Name _____

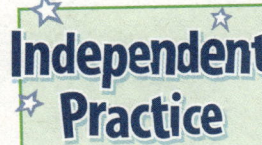
Independent Practice

Circle the object that is longer. Use the orange string to help.

3.   **frog**   **leaf**

4.   **scissors**   **stapler**

5.   **book**   **toothpaste**

6.   **toothpaste**   **stapler**

7. **Higher Order Thinking** Use the objects in Items 5 and 6 to fill in the blanks.

The book is longer than the _____.

The toothpaste is longer than the _____.

So, the book is _____ than the stapler.

Topic 12 | Lesson 2

six hundred seventy-five **675**

Problem Solving
Solve each problem below.

8. **Make Sense** Use the clues to figure out the name of each dog. Write the name under the correct dog.

   Clues
   - Tango is taller than Bongo.
   - Turbo is shorter than Bongo.

Bongo

Turbo

Tango

What's my plan for solving the problem? How can I check that my answer makes sense?

9. **Higher Order Thinking** Josh has two crayons and a piece of string. Explain how he can compare to determine which is the longer crayon without putting the crayons together.

10. **Assessment** Circle the candle holder that is the longest. Use the blue string to help.

676 six hundred seventy-six

Topic 12 | Lesson 2

Name _____

Homework & Practice 12-2
Indirect Measurement

Another Look! You can compare the lengths of 2 objects without putting them next to each other.

"I can use the table to tell if the couch or the bookcase is longer."

The couch is longer than the table.   The bookcase is shorter than the table.

That means the couch is __longer__ than the bookcase.

HOME ACTIVITY Review the meanings of *shorter, shortest, longer, longest* with your child. Put 3 different sized objects on the table. Ask your child to tell you which is the shortest and which is the longest. Then ask him or her if one object is longer than another. Then have your child use the words *longer* and *shorter* to compare all 3 objects.

Circle the object that is shorter. Use the **red** string to help.

1.

2.

Topic 12 | Lesson 2   Digital Resources at SavvasRealize.com   six hundred seventy-seven **677**

Circle the object that is shorter. Use the **purple** string to help.

3.

4.

5.

6.

7. **Higher Order Thinking** Andrea has three candles. Explain how she can use the yellow candle to find out if the red candle is shorter or taller than the blue candle.

8. **Assessment** Circle the shape that is longer. Use the **orange** string to help.

678 six hundred seventy-eight

Topic 12 | Lesson 2

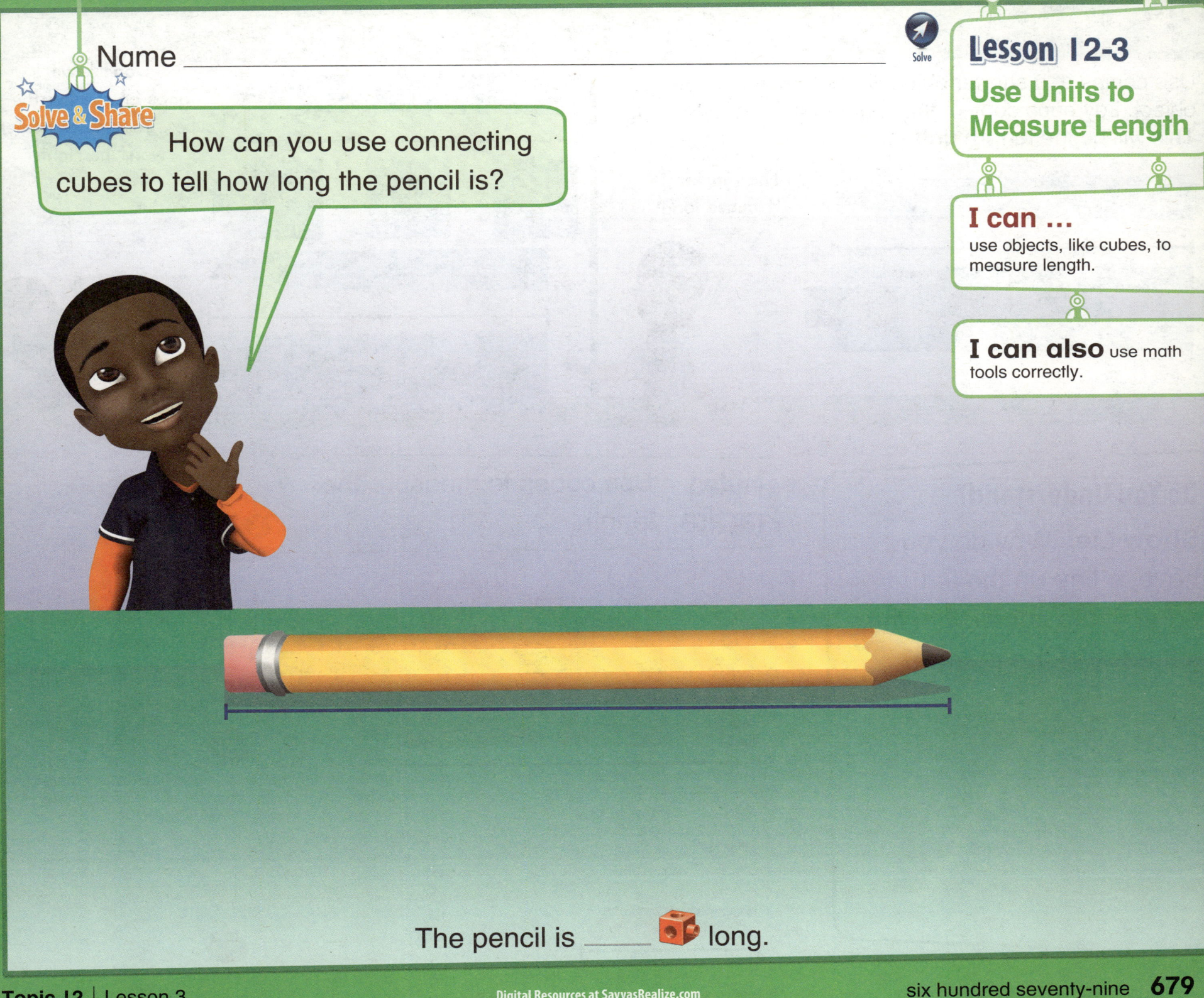

Use copies of a shorter object to **measure** a longer object. Lay each copy of the shorter object end to end. This will be the **length unit**.

The marker is 4 cubes long!

Don't leave gaps or overlap the cubes. Your measurement won't be right.

Do You Understand?

Show Me! Why do you have to line up the left edge of the cubes with the left edge of the marker?

Guided Practice Use cubes to measure the length.

1.

   4

2.

Name _____

Independent Practice Use cubes to measure the length.

3.

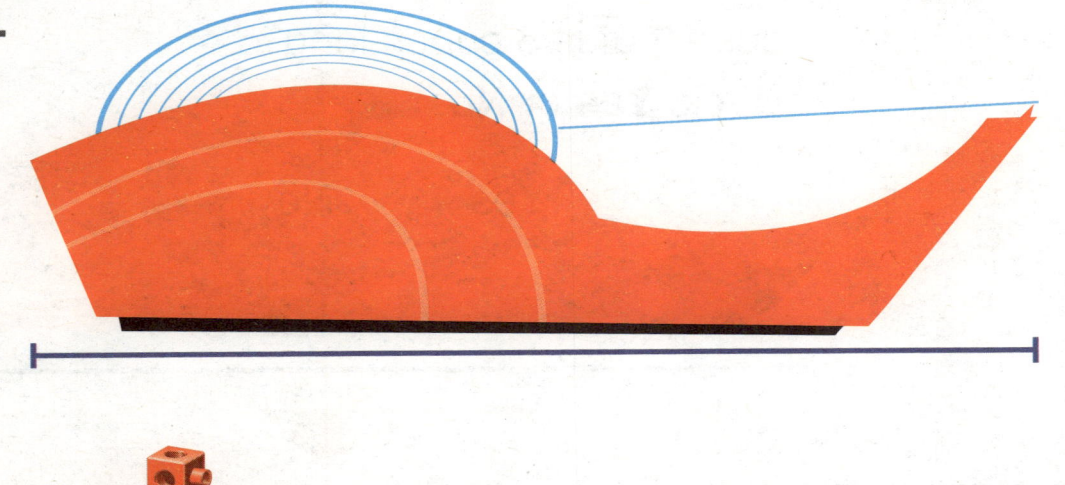

_____

4.

_____

5. **Higher Order Thinking** Measure the length and the height of the calculator. Then tell how much taller the calculator is than it is long.

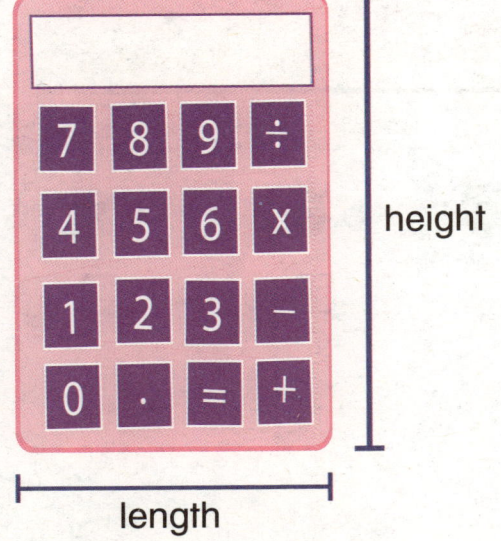

height

length

Measure The  is _____ cubes long.

The  is _____ cubes tall.

The  is _____ cube more than the .

Topic 12 | Lesson 3

six hundred eighty-one **681**

Problem Solving Use cubes to solve each problem below.

6. Use Tools Measure the length of the eraser. Can the eraser fit inside a box that is 4 cubes long?
Circle **Yes** or **No**.

Yes   No

7. Use Tools Measure the length of the paintbrush. Can the paintbrush fit inside a case that is 5 cubes long?
Circle **Yes** or **No**.

Yes   No

8. Higher Order Thinking Find an object that looks like it is about 10 cubes long. Measure the length and the height of the object. Then tell if your object is longer or taller.

Measure:
_____ long _____ tall
My object is _____.

9. Assessment Which is **NOT** the correct length of the marker shown? Choose all that apply.

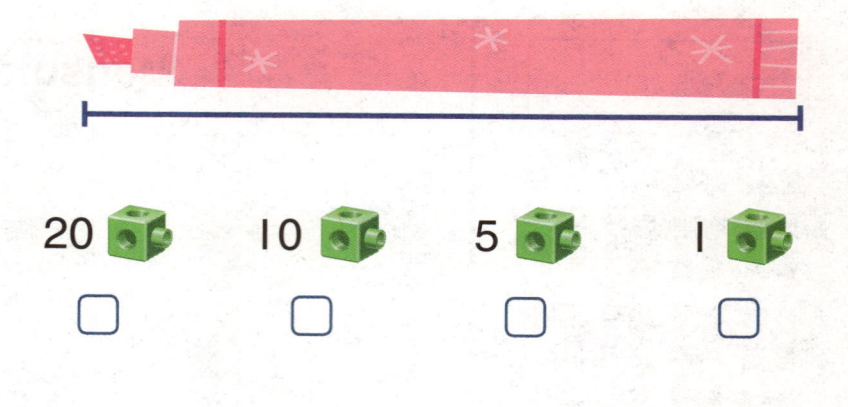

20   10   5   1
☐   ☐   ☐   ☐

Name _____

Homework & Practice 12-3
Use Units to Measure Length

Another Look! You can use smaller objects to measure the length of longer objects. The smaller object will be the length unit.

Use paper clips to measure the length of the book.

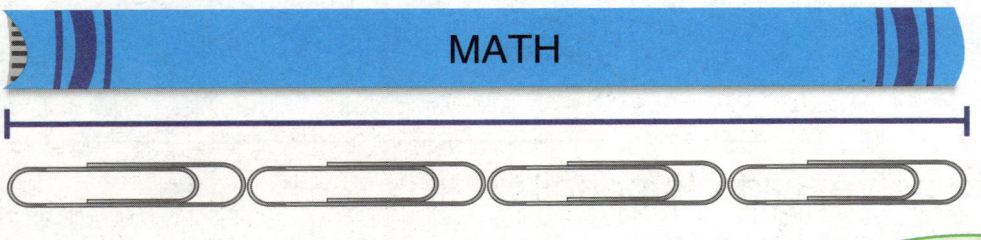

Measure: __4__

Use paper clips that are all the same length. Make sure there are no gaps or overlaps!

HOME ACTIVITY Have your child measure the lengths of several small objects. Use paper clips, or other same-size items, as the length unit.

 Use paper clips to measure the length.

1.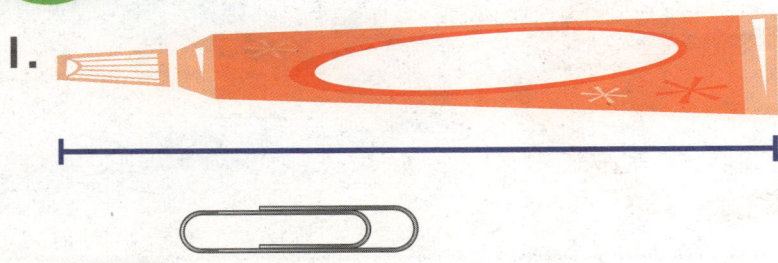
_____

2.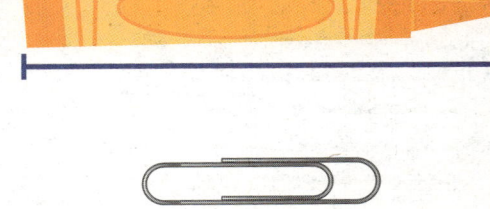
_____

Use paper clips to measure the length.

3.

4.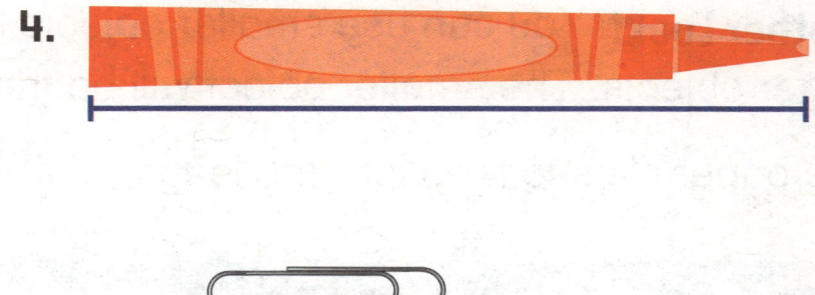

5. **Higher Order Thinking** Draw a picture to solve. Clara's pencil is 5 cubes long. About how long would the pencil be if Clara measured it with paper clips? Explain your answer.

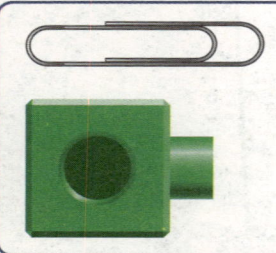

Clara's pencil is about _____ .

6. **Assessment** Which is **NOT** the correct length of the scissors? Choose all that apply.

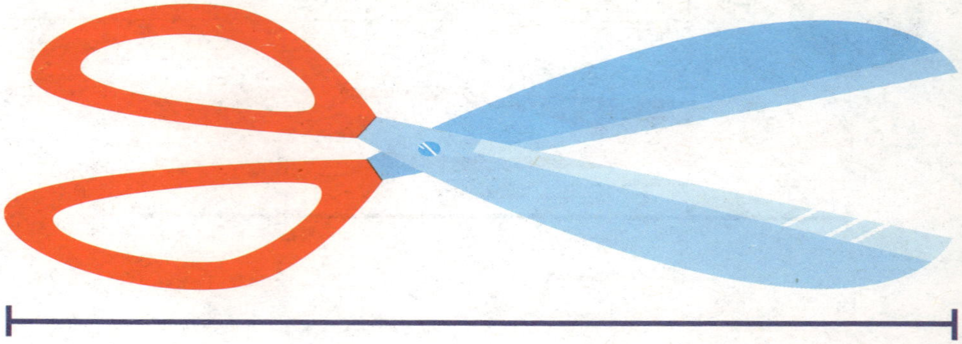

☐ 10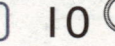
☐ 6
☐ 4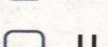
☐ 2

Name _____

Solve & Share

Use cubes to measure the length and the height of the poster. Tell whether the poster is longer or taller. How do you know?

Lesson 12-4
Continue to Measure Length

I can ...
use cubes and other units to compare lengths and heights of objects.

I can also model with math.

The poster is _____ than it is _____.

Topic 12 | Lesson 4

six hundred eighty-five **685**

You can measure objects to compare and order their lengths.

The eraser is about 3  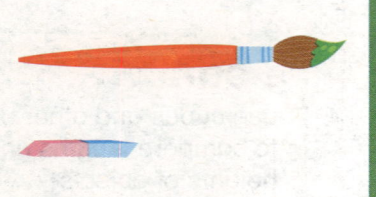 long.
The marker is about 6  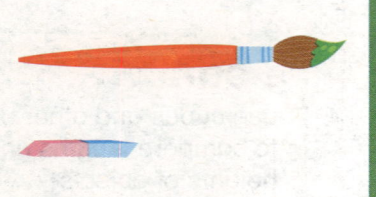 long.

The paintbrush is about 8  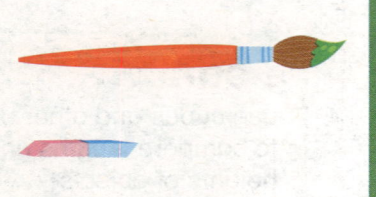 long.

The paintbrush is longer than the marker and the eraser.

The objects are in order from longest to shortest.

longest → 
shortest →

Do You Understand?

Show Me! How do you know which object is shorter? How do you know which object is longer?

Guided Practice

Find each object in your classroom. Measure the length with cubes.

1.  **Bookshelf**
about _____ long

2.  **Desk**
about _____ long

3. The _____ is longer.

686 six hundred eighty-six

Topic 12 | Lesson 4

Name _____

Independent Practice

Find each object in your classroom. Use cubes to measure how tall it is.

4. 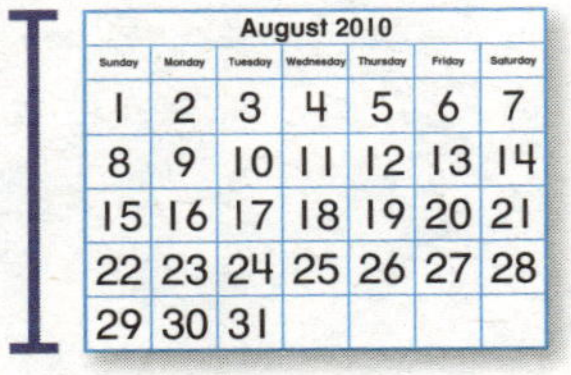 **Calendar**

about _____ 🧊 tall

5. 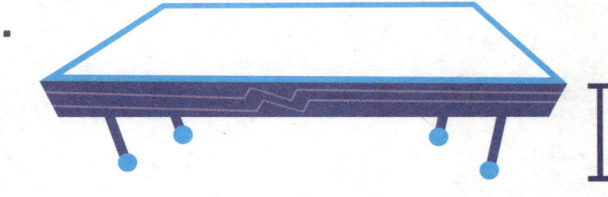 **Table**

about _____ 🧊 tall

6.  **Chair**

about _____ 🧊 tall

7.  **Trash can**

about _____ 🧊 tall

8. **Number Sense** Order the objects from shortest to tallest.

_____   _____   _____   _____
shortest   tallest

Use your measurements above to answer Item 8.

Topic 12 | Lesson 4

six hundred eighty-seven **687**

Problem Solving   Solve the problems below.

9. Model Draw a line that is longer than 2 cubes but shorter than 6 cubes. Then use cubes to measure.

My line is about ____ 🟦 long.

10. Model Draw a tower that is taller than 3 cubes but shorter than 6 cubes. Then use cubes to measure.

My tower is about ____ 🟦 tall.

11. Higher Order Thinking For Item 9, could you have more than one correct answer? Explain.

_____

_____

_____

12. Assessment Measure the green line. Write the number.

The green line is ____ 🟦 long.

688 six hundred eighty-eight

Topic 12 | Lesson 4

Name _____

Homework & Practice 12-4

Continue to Measure Length

Another Look! You can use different objects, such as pennies, to measure.

Measure the length of each object using pennies.

"4 is the greater number, so the duck is the longer object."

HOME ACTIVITY One penny is about $\frac{3}{4}$-inch long/tall. Work with your child to find an object that is approximately 1 penny long or 1 penny tall. Repeat for 2–5 pennies.

about __4__ 🪙 long

about __2__ 🪙 long

Find each object in your house. Measure the length with pennies.

1.  **Shoe**
about _____ 🪙 long

2.  **Shirt**
about _____ 🪙 long

3. 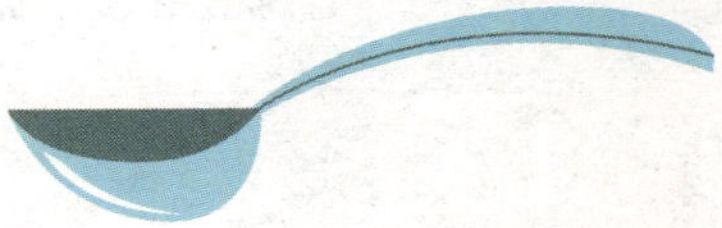 **Spoon**
about _____ 🪙 long

Topic 12 | Lesson 4

Find each object in your house. Measure the length with pennies.

4.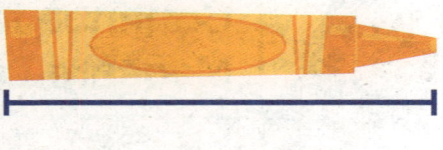

5.

6.

about _____  long

about _____  long

about _____ tall

7. **Higher Order Thinking** Which of the objects above is the longest? Which is the shortest? Explain how you know.

_____
_____
_____
_____
_____

8. ✓ **Assessment** Measure the height of the rectangle. Write the number.

The rectangle is _____ tall.

Name _____

Solve & Share

Which tool or tools would you use to measure the length of the ribbon? Tell why.

Measure the ribbon. Then circle the tools you used.

Problem Solving

Lesson 12-5
Use Appropriate Tools

I can ...
choose an appropriate tool and use it to measure a given object.

I can also measure straight and crooked objects.

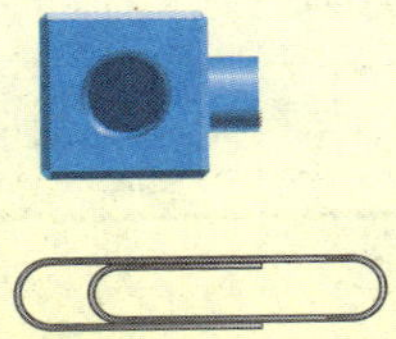

Thinking Habits
Which tools can I use?

Is there a different tool I could use?

Measure

about _____

Topic 12 | Lesson 5 · Digital Resources at SavvasRealize.com · six hundred ninety-one **691**

How can you measure an object that is **not** straight?

Which tools can I use?

I can use paper clips, cubes, string, or more than one tool!

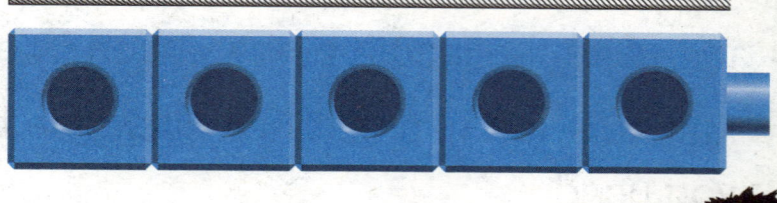

You can straighten the string and then measure its length with cubes.

The snake is about 5 cubes long.

Do You Understand?

Show Me! Why might you need more than one tool to measure the length of a curvy object?

Guided Practice

Circle whether you need just cubes or string and cubes to measure each object. Then measure.

1. cubes   (string and cubes)

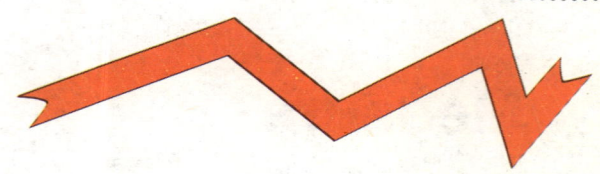

about __4__ cubes

2. cubes   string and cubes

about ____ cubes

692 six hundred ninety-two

Topic 12 | Lesson 5

Name _____

Independent Practice Circle whether you need just cubes or string and cubes to measure each object. Then measure.

3. cubes   string and cubes

_____ cubes

4. cubes   string and cubes

_____ cubes

5. cubes   string and cubes

_____ cubes

6. cubes   string and cubes

_____ cubes

Topic 12 | Lesson 5

six hundred ninety-three **693**

Problem Solving

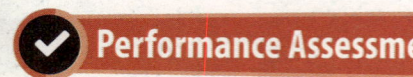

Hanging Bracelets

Kate needs to hang these bracelets in order from shortest to longest.

7. **Use Tools** Circle the set of tools that Kate should use to measure.

   cubes   cubes and string

8. **Explain** Explain why the tools you chose will give the most accurate measurement.

   _____

   _____

   _____

9. **Use Tools** Measure each bracelet. Then write the colors of the bracelets in order from shortest to longest.

   _____ , _____ , _____

694 six hundred ninety-four

Name _____

Homework & Practice 12-5
Use Appropriate Tools

Another Look! First use string to measure the ribbon.

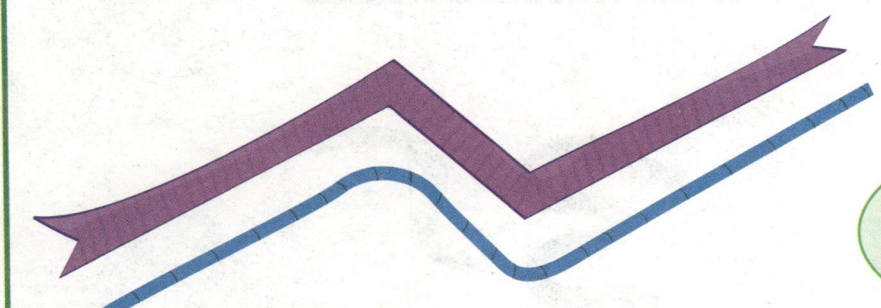

Then use paper clips to measure the string.

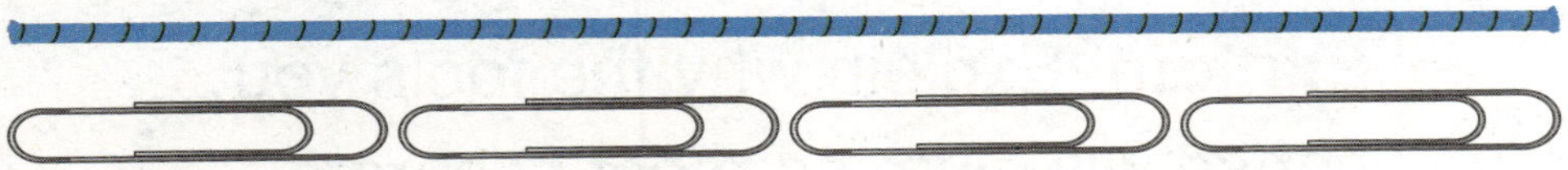

The string measures 4 paper clips long.

So, the ribbon is about ___4___ paper clips long.

A string is a good tool to use when you measure an object that isn't straight.

HOME ACTIVITY Place a shoelace or piece of string on the table in a curved position (not straight). Ask your child to use cubes (or objects of similar size) to measure the length of the string without straightening it. Then straighten the string and ask your child to measure again. Discuss the difference in the measurements and the reason for this difference.

Circle whether you need just paper clips or string and paper clips to measure each object. Then measure.

1. paper clips   string and paper clips

___ paper clips

2. paper clips   string and paper clips

___ paper clips

Topic 12 | Lesson 5 — six hundred ninety-five **695**

Performance Assessment

Race Courses

Pete ran races on 3 different courses. Help him put the courses in order from shortest to longest.

1

2   3

3. **Use Tools** Which tools would you use to measure each race course? Would you use the same tools to measure each course? Explain your choice.

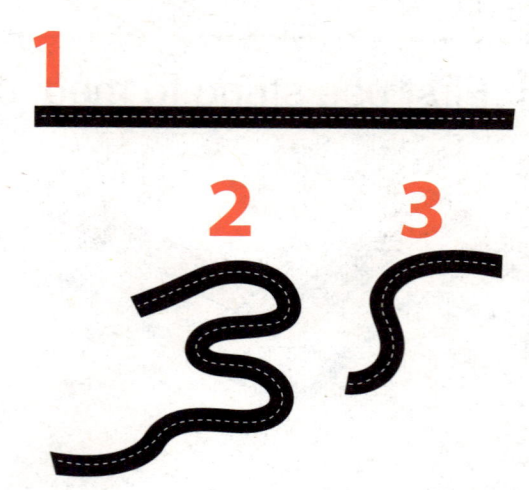

_____
_____
_____

4. **Explain** Explain why the tools you chose will give the most accurate measurement.

_____
_____
_____

5. **Use Tools** Measure each course. Then write the numbers of the courses in order from shortest to longest.

____, ____, ____

696 six hundred ninety-six

Name _____

Find a Match

Find a partner. Point to a clue. Read the clue.

Look below the clues to find a match. Write the clue letter in the box next to the match.

Find a match for every clue.

TOPIC 12 Fluency Practice Activity

I can ...
add and subtract within 10.

Clues

A 8 + 1

B 4 + 4

C 8 − 3

D 8 − 7

E 8 − 1

F 1 + 1

G 4 + 2

H 1 + 3

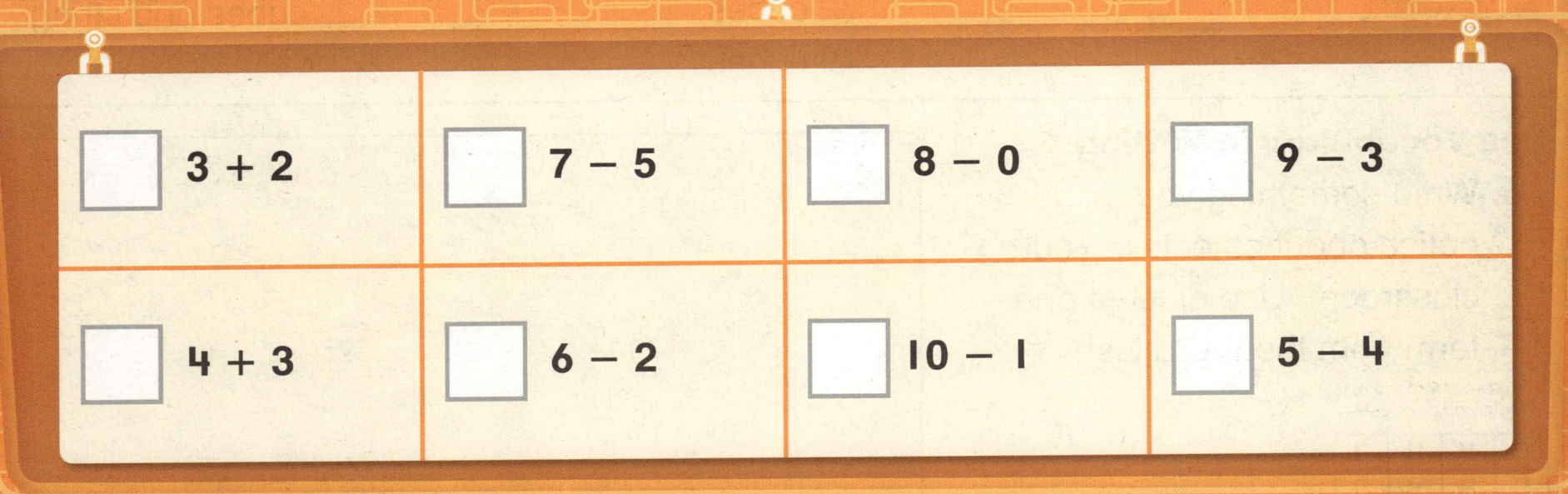

| ☐ 3 + 2 | ☐ 7 − 5 | ☐ 8 − 0 | ☐ 9 − 3 |
| ☐ 4 + 3 | ☐ 6 − 2 | ☐ 10 − 1 | ☐ 5 − 4 |

Topic 12 | Fluency Practice Activity

Answers for Find a Match on next page.

six hundred ninety-seven 697

TOPIC 12 Vocabulary Review

Word List
- length
- length unit
- longer
- measure
- shorter
- shortest

Understand Vocabulary

1. Fill in the blank.

   I can use _____ to _____ to find out how long something is.

2. Fill in the blank.

   The _____ object is the one with the smallest measurement.

3. Circle the lines that are longer than this one. _____

   _____

   _____

4. Cross out the measurement that is **NOT** shorter than 19 cubes.

   8 cubes
   32 cubes
   14 cubes

5. Cross out the tool that can **NOT** be used to measure length.

   cubes
   number chart
   cubes and string

Use Vocabulary in Writing

6. Write something you notice about objects in your classroom. Use at least one term from the Word List.

Name _____

Set A

You can find the object that is the longest.

← longest

← shortest

You can also find the object that is the shortest.

Reteaching

Circle the longest line in each group. Draw a box around the shortest line in each group.

1.

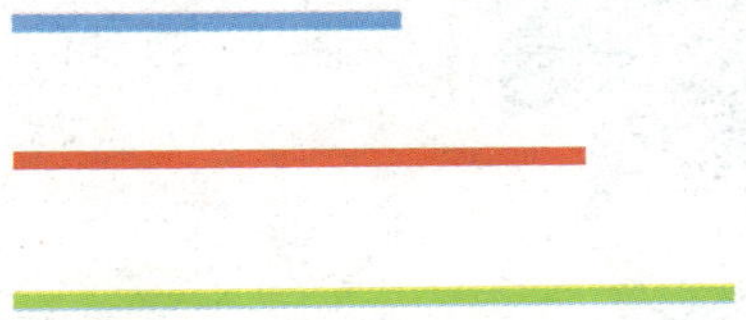

2.

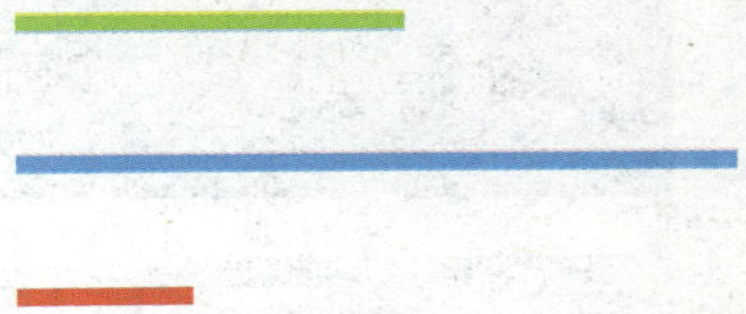

Set B

You can compare the lengths of two objects that are not lined up next to each other by using a third object.

The paper clip is shorter than the eraser. The pencil is longer than the eraser. So, the pencil is longer than the paper clip.

Circle the object that is longer. Use the red object to help.

3.

4.

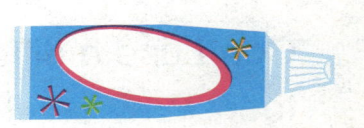

Topic 12 | Reteaching

six hundred ninety-nine 699

Set C

You can measure the length of an object in cubes.

The marker is about 4 cubes

Use cubes to measure.

5.

The green strip is about ____ cubes

6.

The blue strip is about ____ cubes

Lay the cubes end to end. Don't leave gaps between them or let them overlap.

Set D

Thinking Habits
Use Tools

What tool can I use to help solve the problem?

Can I use a different tool? Why or why not?

Choose the tool or tools you can use to measure the object. Then measure the length.

7. cubes   cubes and string

____ cubes

Name _____

TOPIC 12 Assessment

1. Circle the tool or tools you would use to measure the length of the picture. Then explain why you chose that tool or tools.

   cubes   string and cubes

   _____
   _____
   _____
   _____
   _____

2. Which word describes the red line?

   shortest   middle   tallest   longest
      Ⓐ   Ⓑ   Ⓒ   Ⓓ

3. Use cubes to measure the height of the notebook.

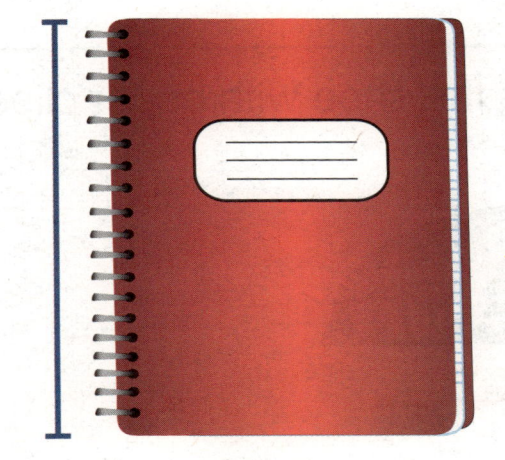

   ____ high

Topic 12 | Assessment

seven hundred one   701

4. Use cubes to measure the length of the feather.

Ⓐ 2
Ⓑ 6
Ⓒ 4
Ⓓ 8

5. Measure the blue, red, and yellow lines with cubes. Which sentences are true about the lines? Choose all that apply.

☐ The blue line is shortest.
☐ The red line is shortest.
☐ The blue line is longer than the yellow line.
☐ The yellow line is longer than the blue line.

Circle the object that is shorter. Use the red object to help.

6.

7.

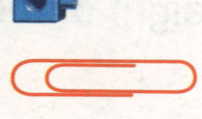

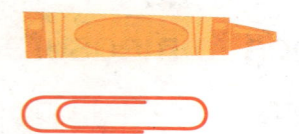

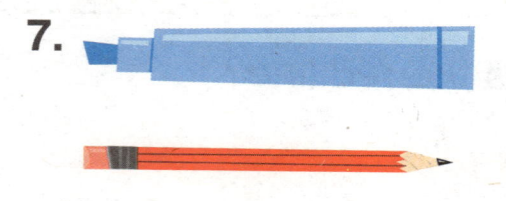

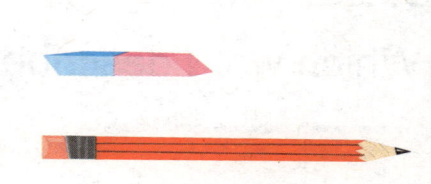

8. Tom measures the shoe with paper clips. Did Tom measure correctly? Explain.

_____
_____
_____

Name _____

School Supplies

Sally uses many different supplies at school.

1. Which pencil is the longest?
   Circle that color.
   Which pencil is the shortest?
   Cross out that color.

   yellow   red   blue

2. Which object is longer? Circle that object. Use the orange object to help.

Topic 12 | Performance Assessment

seven hundred three **703**

3. Use cubes. Measure the length of the chalk. _____ cubes

Sally says that the chalk would fit inside of a box that is 6 cubes long.
Do you agree with her? Circle **Yes** or **No**.   **Yes**   **No**
Explain your answer.

_____
_____
_____

4. Sally uses these two ribbons for her art project.

Part A
Use string and cubes to measure the length of each ribbon.

about _____ cubes   about _____ cubes

Part B
How much longer is the purple ribbon than the pink ribbon?

about _____ cubes longer

TOPIC 13 Time

Essential Question: What are different ways to tell time?

Musical instruments can make many different sounds.

Almost all of these sounds are made when some part of the instrument vibrates.

Wow! Let's do this project and learn more.

Math and Science Project: The Sound of Vibration

Find Out Talk to friends and relatives about the sounds that different musical instruments make. Ask them if they know what part of the instrument vibrates to make the sound.

Journal: Make a Book Show what you found out. In your book, also:
- Draw pictures of different musical instruments.
- Circle or highlight the part of the instrument that vibrates to make a sound.

Name _____

Review What You Know

Vocabulary

1. **Count** to find the missing numbers.

    28, 29, __30__, __31__, 32, __33__, 34, __35__

2. Circle the number in the **ones** place.

    1 (2)

3. Write the missing numbers to complete the **pattern**.

Tens	Ones
3	3
1	
	33

Counting

4. Count by 1s to write the missing numbers.

    47, 48, ____, ____, ____, 52, 53, ____

5. Count by 10s to write the missing numbers.

    ____, 20, 30, ____, ____, ____

Use Tools to Count

6. Use what you know about counting on a hundred chart to fill in the missing numbers.

    | 31 | 32 | 33 | 34 | 35 | 36 | 37 | 38 | 39 | 40 |
    | 41 | 42 | 43 | 44 | | 46 | 47 | 48 | 49 | 50 |
    | 51 | 52 | 53 | 54 | | 56 | 57 | 58 | 59 | 60 |

My Word Cards Study the words on the front of the card. Complete the activity on the back.

hour hand

hour hand

hour

An **hour** is 60 minutes.

2:00

minute hand

minute hand

minute

60 **minutes** is 1 hour.

o'clock

8:00

8 o'clock

half hour

A **half hour** is 30 minutes.

1:30

Topic 13 | My Word Cards

seven hundred seven **707**

My Word Cards — Use what you know to complete the sentences. Extend learning by writing your own sentence using each word.

The __minute hand__ is the long hand on a clock.

There are 60 minutes in 1 __hour__.

The __hour hand__ is the short hand on a clock.

There are 30 minutes in a __half hour__.

3:00 is read as 3 __o'clock__.

There are 60 __minutes__ in 1 hour.

Name _____

Solve & Share

Draw a picture to show how you would tell time without clocks.

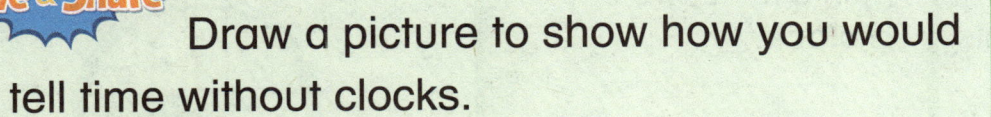

Then tell a partner whether we need clocks or don't need clocks.

Lesson 13-1
Understand the Hour and Minute Hands

I can ...
tell time to the hour.

I can also make sense of problems.

Topic 13 | Lesson 1

seven hundred nine **709**

The short hand is the **hour hand**. The hour hand tells us what **hour** it is.

hour hand

The long hand is the **minute hand**. The minute hand points to the **minute**.

minute hand

When the minute hand points to 12, we say **o'clock**.

This clock shows 3 o'clock.

The hour hand is on 3. The minute hand is on 12.

Do You Understand?

Show Me! How is the hour hand different from the minute hand?

Guided Practice

Write the time shown on each clock.

1. hour hand: 4
   minute hand: 12
   4 o'clock

2. hour hand: ___
   minute hand: ___
   ___ o'clock

3. hour hand: ___
   minute hand: ___
   ___ o'clock

710 seven hundred ten

Topic 13 | Lesson 1

Name _____

Independent Practice Draw the hour and minute hands to show the time.

4. 10 o'clock

5. 2 o'clock

6. 11 o'clock

7. 12 o'clock

8. 6 o'clock

9. 1 o'clock

10. 5 o'clock

11. 8 o'clock

12. **Higher Order Thinking** Write a time.
Draw the hour and minute hands to show the time.
Draw a picture to show an activity you do at that time.

____ o'clock

Topic 13 | Lesson 1

seven hundred eleven 711

Problem Solving Solve each problem below.

13. Look for Patterns Sarah wakes up at 7 o'clock. Draw the hands on the clock to show 7 o'clock.

14. Math and Science Each string on a guitar makes a different sound when it vibrates. Joe starts tuning his guitar at 9 o'clock. It takes him one hour to finish. What time does he finish?

_____ o'clock

15. Higher Order Thinking Karen starts playing soccer one hour after 5 o'clock. Draw the hour and minute hands on the clock to show what time Karen starts playing soccer.

Then write a sentence about an activity you might do at that time.

16. Assessment Bill likes to read after 3 o'clock and before 5 o'clock. Which clock shows the time Bill might read?

Ⓐ   Ⓑ

Ⓒ   Ⓓ

Name _____

Homework & Practice 13-1
Understand the Hour and Minute Hands

Another Look! You can use the hands on a clock to tell time. The short hand is the hour hand. The long hand is the minute hand.

The hour hand points to 6.

The minute hand points to 12.

It is 6 o'clock.

The hour hand points to 3.

The minute hand points to 12.

It is 3 o'clock.

HOME ACTIVITY Using an analog clock in your home, help your child make a list of activities they do on a given day. Have him or her write the time that each activity begins.

Write the time shown on each clock.

1. hour hand: _____
   minute hand: _____
   _____ o'clock

2. hour hand: _____
   minute hand: _____
   _____ o'clock

3. hour hand: _____
   minute hand: _____
   _____ o'clock

Draw hour hands and minute hands to show the time.

4. 10 o'clock

5. 2 o'clock

6. 11 o'clock

7. 3 o'clock

8. 9 o'clock

9. 6 o'clock

Solve each problem below.

10. **Higher Order Thinking** Write a good time for eating lunch. Then draw an hour hand and a minute hand to show the time.

_____ o'clock

11. **Assessment** Every Saturday, Rachel wakes up after 6 o'clock and before 9 o'clock. Which tells the time Rachel might wake up every Saturday?

Ⓐ 2 o'clock
Ⓑ 4 o'clock
Ⓒ 5 o'clock
Ⓓ 8 o'clock

Name _____

Solve & Share

Both of the clocks show the same time. Tell what time is shown. Then write one way the clocks are alike and one way they are different.

Lesson 13-2
Tell and Write Time to the Hour

I can ...
tell time to the hour using 2 different types of clock.

I can also reason about math.

___ o'clock

Alike	Different

Topic 13 | Lesson 2   Digital Resources at SavvasRealize.com   seven hundred fifteen **715**

I eat breakfast at 7 o'clock.

This clock shows 7 o'clock.

This clock shows 7 o'clock another way.

7 tells the hour. 00 tells the minutes.

7 o'clock is the same as 7:00.

Do You Understand?

Show Me! Do the clocks show the same time? Explain.

Guided Practice Draw the hands on the clock face. Then write the time on the other clock.

1. 3 o'clock
2. 5 o'clock
3. 12 o'clock
4. 11 o'clock

716 seven hundred sixteen

Topic 13 | Lesson 2

Name _____

Independent Practice

Draw the hands on the clock face.
Then write the time on the other clock.

5.  2 o'clock

6.  4 o'clock

7.  6 o'clock

8.  9 o'clock

9.  10 o'clock

10.  1 o'clock

Think about how hands move on a clock to help solve the problem.

11. Number Sense Mary writes a pattern. Then she erases some of the times. Write the missing times.

6:00, 8:00, ____:____, 12:00, ____:____

Topic 13 | Lesson 2

seven hundred seventeen **717**

Problem Solving

Solve each problem below.

12. **Reasoning** Raul starts riding his bike at 1:00. He rides for 1 hour.
What time does Raul stop?
Draw the hands on the clock face.
Then write the time on the other clock.

13. **Vocabulary** Lucy reads for 1 **hour**. She stops reading at 10:00.
What time did Lucy start reading?
Draw the hands on the clock face.
Then write the **hour** Lucy starts reading.

_____ o'clock

14. **Higher Order Thinking** David goes to bed 2 hours before his mother. David's mother goes to bed at 11:00.

Write the time David goes to bed on the clock.

15. **Assessment** Maribel washes dishes after 6:00 and before 9:00. Which clocks show a time Maribel might wash dishes? Choose all that apply.

12:00 ☐   8:00 ☐

7:00 ☐   5:00 ☐

718 seven hundred eighteen · Topic 13 | Lesson 2

Name: carter calloway 2-9-2022

Homework & Practice 13-2
Tell and Write Time to the Hour

Another Look! Both clocks show the same time.

4 tells the hour.
00 tells the minutes.
Both clocks show 4 o'clock.

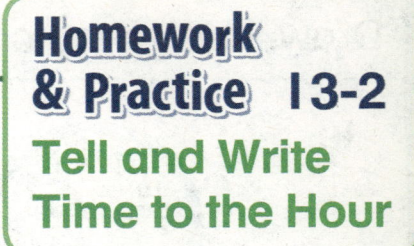

_7_ tells the hour.
_00_ tells the minutes.
Both clocks show _7_ o'clock.

HOME ACTIVITY Use a digital clock in your home to help your child practice telling time. When your child is doing an activity on the hour, ask him or her to tell you the time. Repeat with other times and other activities.

Draw the hands on the clock face. Then write the time on the other clock.

1. 3:00 — 3 o'clock

2. 7:00 — 7 o'clock

3. 10:00 — 10 o'clock

Topic 13 | Lesson 2 seven hundred nineteen 719

Draw lines to match the clocks that show the same time.

4. 1:00 — 3:00

5. 12:00 — 9:00

6. 5:00 — 6:00

7. Higher Order Thinking Write a good time for eating dinner.

Draw hands on the clock face to show the time. Then write the time on the other clock.

5 : 00

__5__ o'clock

8. Assessment Look at the time on the clock face. Which clocks below do **NOT** show the same time? Choose all that apply.

10:00 ☒   8:00 ☒   7:00 ☒   4:00 ☑

720 seven hundred twenty

Name _____

Solve & Share

The red clock shows a time to the hour. The blue clock is missing its minute hand.

Draw the minute hand on the blue clock so the clock shows a half hour later. Tell why you think you are right.

Lesson 13-3
Tell and Write Time to the Half Hour

I can ...
tell time to the half hour.

I can also reason about math.

Topic 13 | Lesson 3

Digital Resources at SavvasRealize.com

seven hundred twenty-one 721

When the minute hand is on 6, we can say 30 or half past the hour.

"The hour hand is halfway between the 2 and 3."

It is half past 2 or 2:30.

"An hour is 60 minutes. A half hour is 30 minutes."

Do You Understand?

Show Me! Why is the hour hand between 6 and 7 when it is 6:30?

Guided Practice Write the numbers to complete each sentence. Then write the time on the other clock.

1. The hour hand is between __7__ and __8__.

   The minute hand is on __6__.

   7:30

2. The hour hand is between ____ and ____.

   The minute hand is on ____.

722 seven hundred twenty-two

Topic 13 | Lesson 3

Name _____

Independent Practice Write the time shown on each clock.

3.  　　　　　　　　　　　　4.   　　　　　　　　　　　　5.

Look at the pattern. Write the missing times.

6. 6:00, 6:30, 7:00, _____, 8:00, _____, _____

7. 2:30, 3:30, _____, 5:30, _____, _____

8. **Higher Order Thinking** Carlos plays basketball for 30 minutes each day. He always starts playing at half past an hour. Write times he might start and stop playing basketball. Draw the hands on each clock face to show the times.

START 　　　　　　　　　　**STOP**

___:___　　　　　　　　　　___:___

Topic 13 | Lesson 3　　　　　　　　　　　　　　seven hundred twenty-three **723**

Problem Solving Solve each problem below.

9. Be Precise Sandy walks her dog at 3:00. She walks for 30 minutes. What time does Sandy stop walking her dog? Draw the hands on the clock face. Write the time on the other clock.

10. Be Precise Robin gets to school at 9:00. Her math class starts 30 minutes later. What time does Robin's math class start? Draw the hands on the clock face. Write the time on the other clock.

11. Higher Order Thinking Show 8:00 on the first clock. On the second clock, show the time 30 minutes later. Is the hour hand still on 8? Explain.

12. Assessment Which clock below shows the same time as the clock face?

Ⓐ 12:30   Ⓑ 1:30   Ⓒ 2:30   Ⓓ 3:30

Name carter calloway

Homework & Practice 13-3
Tell and Write Time to the Half Hour

Another Look! Clocks can tell us the time to the half hour.
A half hour is 30 minutes.

The hour hand is between 7 and 8.
The minute hand is on 6.
It is 7:30.

The hour hand is between __11__ and __12__.
The minute hand is on __6__.
It is __11:30__.

HOME ACTIVITY Using an analog clock, have your child practice telling the time to the half hour. If possible, have him or her move the hands on the clock to tell the time you say. For example, say, "Show me 6:30." Have your child write the time on a sheet of paper after telling the time.

Complete the sentences. Then write the time on the other clock.

1. 3:30

The hour hand is between __3__ and __4__.
The minute hand is on __6__.
It is __3:30__.

2. 8:30

The hour hand is between __8__ and __10__.
The minute hand is on __6__.
It is __8:30__.

Topic 13 | Lesson 3   Digital Resources at SavvasRealize.com   seven hundred twenty-five **725**

3. **Explain** It takes Vanessa a half hour to walk to the library. She leaves her house at 5:00. What time does she get to the library?

Write the time on the clock. Then explain how you solved.

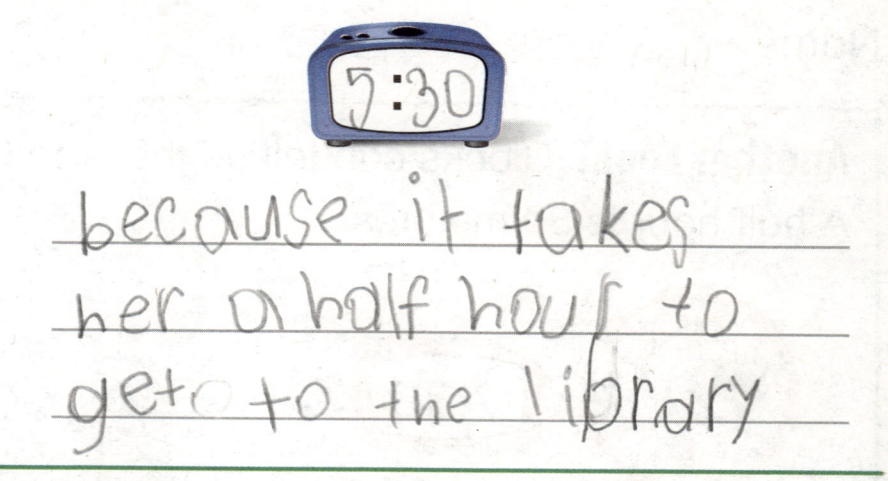

5:30

because it takes her a half hour to geto to the library

4. **Algebra** Kirk stirs his soup at 1:00. He started cooking the soup 30 minutes earlier. What time did Kirk start cooking his soup? Draw the hands on the clock face and write the time.

12 : 30

5. **Higher Order Thinking** Write about something you do a half hour before bedtime. Write the time on the clock. Draw the hands on the clock face to show the time.

7:30

I watch tv.

6. **Assessment** Which shows the same time as the clock face?

8:30   8:00   7:30   6:30

Ⓐ   Ⓑ   Ⓒ   Ⓓ

Name _____

Solve & Share

Noel has a music lesson at 3:30. At 4:30, he goes to the library. He gets ready at 5:00 so he can have dinner at 5:30. After dinner ends at 6:00, he plays a game. How can you organize this information in a schedule?

Afternoon Schedule

Time	Activity

Problem Solving

Lesson 13-4
Reasoning

I can ... use reasoning to tell and write time.

I can also read and use a schedule.

Thinking Habits

What do the numbers stand for?

How are the numbers in the problem related?

Mr. Diaz starts to read a story halfway between 8:00 and 9:00. What time does Mr. Diaz start the story? Show the hands on the clock.

Mr. Diaz's Class Schedule

Time	Activity
8:00	Reading
9:00	Math
10:00	Recess
10:30	Art
11:30	Lunch

How can I make sense of the question?

What does "halfway" mean?

What is my thinking?

The time between 8:00 and 9:00 is one hour, or 60 minutes. A half hour is 30 minutes.

8:30 is halfway between 8:00 and 9:00. I can look back at the table to see if my answer makes sense.

Do You Understand?

Show Me! What happens 1 hour after Art begins? Explain how you know.

Guided Practice Use Mr. Diaz's Class Schedule above to answer the questions. Circle the activity that starts at the time shown. Then explain your reasoning.

1.  Recess / Art / (Reading)

2.  10:30 — Art / Recess / Lunch

728 seven hundred twenty-eight

Topic 13 | Lesson 4

Name _____

Independent Practice Use the Nature Trip Schedule to answer the questions.

3. Which activity do children do just before the Bird Watch? Explain your reasoning.

   _____
   _____

4. Which activity or activities do children do after Lunch? Explain your reasoning.

   _____
   _____

5. Which activity starts at the time shown? Explain your reasoning.

   _____
   _____

Nature Trip Schedule	
Time	**Activity**
10:00	Walk
11:00	Bird Watch
12:00	Lunch
12:30	Make a Birdhouse
1:30	Pick Flowers

6. **Vocabulary** Circle the time that shows a **half hour** past 3:00.

   2:00   3:00   3:30   4:00

Topic 13 | Lesson 4   seven hundred twenty-nine **729**

Problem Solving

✓ **Performance Assessment**

Visiting the City Andrew's family takes a day trip to the city.

Help him solve problems using the Family Schedule.

Family Schedule

Time	Activity
10:00	Museum
12:30	Aquarium
2:00	City Tour
4:30	C Building
5:30	Dinner

7. **Model** The minute hand fell off this clock. What time should the clock show when Andrew's family arrives at the Aquarium?

Draw the minute hand and write the time shown.

8. **Reasoning** Andrew writes down all the activities his family is doing at 30 minutes after the hour. How many activities did Andrew write? Explain how you found out.

_____

_____

_____

730 seven hundred thirty   Topic 13 | Lesson 4

Name _____

Homework & Practice 13-4
Reasoning

Another Look! You can use reasoning to solve problems about time.

Mr. K's students can work with a partner for the second half of Writing.

What time can students start working with a partner?

How are the numbers related? How can you use what you know to solve?

Students can start working with a partner at **1:30**.

Class Schedule

Time	Class
12:30	Silent Reading
1:00	Writing
2:00	P.E.

What time is halfway between 1:00 and 2:00? I know 1:00 to 2:00 is 1 hour. I know a half hour is 30 minutes. 30 minutes after 1:00 is 1:30.

HOME ACTIVITY Help your child create a schedule for a typical school day. Ask questions about the schedule, such as, "What time do you eat lunch?" or "What time is a half hour after Math?"

Use the schedule above to solve the problems below.

1. Draw the hands on the clock to show when Silent Reading begins. Then explain your reasoning.

2. What time is it 30 minutes after P.E. starts? Write the correct time on the clock. Then explain your reasoning.

Topic 13 | Lesson 4

seven hundred thirty-one **731**

✓ **Performance Assessment**

Fun Run Gina's school is hosting a fundraiser for music programs. Can you use the schedule to help solve problems about the fundraiser?

Use your understanding of telling and writing time to solve the problems.

| Fundraiser Schedule ||
Time	Activity
10:00	Introductions
10:30	Auction
11:30	Fun Run
2:00	Closing Speech

3. **Model** What time do the introductions start at the fundraiser? Write the correct time on the clock to show your answer.

4. **Reasoning** Gina drew the hands on this clock to show the time the Closing Speech starts. Is she correct? If not, draw the correct hands on the clock at the right.

732 seven hundred thirty-two

Point & Tally

Name _____

TOPIC 13 Fluency Practice Activity

Find a partner. Get paper and a pencil.
Each partner chooses a different color: light blue or dark blue.
Partner 1 and Partner 2 each point to a black number at the same time. Both partners add those numbers.
If the answer is on your color, you get a tally mark.
Work until one partner gets twelve tally marks.

I can ...
add and subtract within 10.

Partner 1: 8, 6, 0, 7, 3, 5

| 0 | 6 | 10 | 9 | 3 | 8 |
| 1 | 7 | 2 | 4 | 0 | 5 |

Partner 2: 0, 1, 2, 1, 0, 2

Tally Marks for Partner 1

Tally Marks for Partner 2

Topic 13 | Fluency Practice Activity

seven hundred thirty-three 733

TOPIC 13 Vocabulary Review

Word List
- half hour
- hour
- hour hand
- minute
- minute hand
- o'clock

Understand Vocabulary

1. Circle the hour hand.

2. Circle the minute hand.

3. Fill in the blank. Use a word from the Word List.
   30 minutes is a _____.

4. Fill in the blank. Use a word from the Word List.
   In the time 8:30, 8 is the _____.

5. Fill in the blank. Use a word from the Word List.
   In the time 8:30, 30 is the _____.

Use Vocabulary in Writing

6. Tell what time is shown on the clock using a word from the Word List.

   10:00

Name _____

Set A

You can draw the hour and minute hands to show the time.

minute hand
hour hand
8 o'clock

When the minute hand points to 12, you say o'clock.

Reteaching

TOPIC 13

Draw the hour and minute hands to show the time.

1. 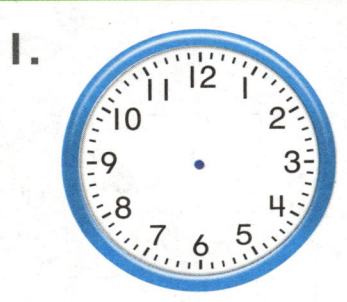 3 o'clock

2.  11 o'clock

Set B

What time does the clock show?

5 shows the hour.
00 shows the minutes.

5:00

_5_ o'clock

Write the time shown on each clock.

3.  6:00
____ o'clock

4.  10:00
____ o'clock

Topic 13 | Reteaching

seven hundred thirty-five **735**

Set C

What time do the clocks show?

half past __8__

or __8__ : __30__

Remember: Half past means 30 minutes after the hour.

Write the time shown on each clock.

5. half past _____

or _____ : _____

6. half past _____

or _____ : _____

Set D

Thinking Habits

Reasoning

What do the numbers stand for?

How are the numbers in the problem related?

Use the schedule to answer the questions.

| Mr. Diaz's Class Schedule ||
Time	Activity
8:30	Reading
9:30	Math
10:30	Recess

7. What activity starts 2 hours after Reading?

_____

8. What time does Math begin?

_____ : _____

Name ______________________________

1. Lisa rides her bike after 2 o'clock and before 6 o'clock every Friday. Which clocks show the time Lisa might ride her bike? Choose all that apply.

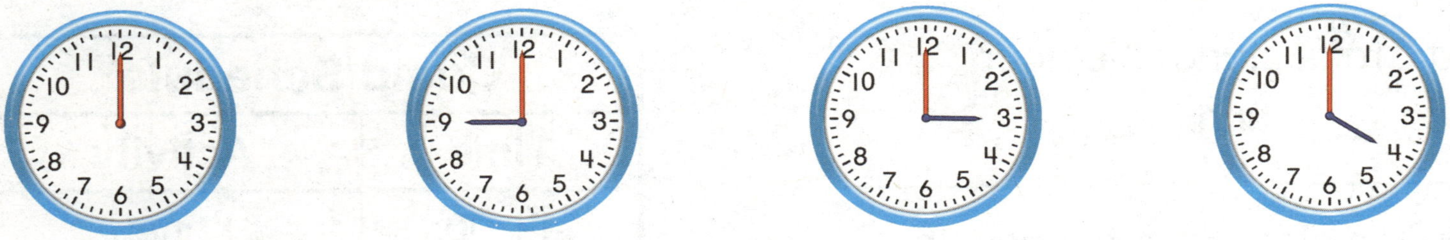

☐ ☐ ☐ ☐

2. Which clock shows the same time as the clock face?

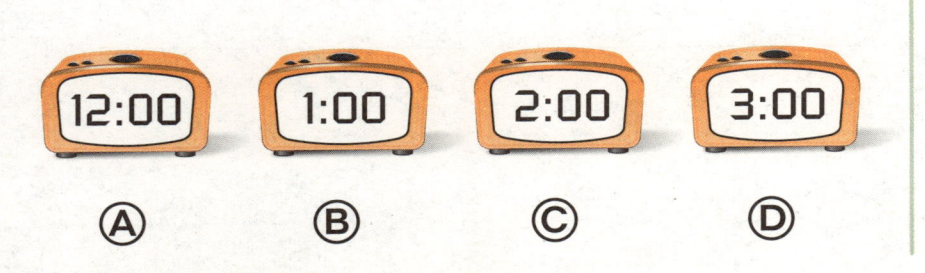

12:00
1:00
2:00
3:00

Ⓐ Ⓑ Ⓒ Ⓓ

3. Write the time that is shown on the clock face.

:

4. How many minutes are in a half hour?

15	20	30	60
Ⓐ	Ⓑ	Ⓒ	Ⓓ

5. Write the numbers to complete the sentence.

   When Arts and Crafts starts, the hour hand is between _____ and _____.

Camp Schedule	
Time	Activity
11:00	Lunch
12:00	Swimming
1:30	Story Time
2:00	Snack Time
2:30	Arts and Crafts

6. Draw hands on the clock face to show the time that Story Time starts.

7. Show the same time on both clocks. How do you know you are correct?

738 seven hundred thirty-eight

Name _____

A Trip to the Zoo

Carol and her class take a trip to the zoo. The chart shows their schedule.

Zoo Schedule	
Time	Activity
9:00	Bird House
9:30	Train Ride
10:00	Large Animals
11:30	Lunch
12:30	Dolphin Show
1:00	Small Animals

1. Show another way to write the time for each activity.

   Large Animals _____

   Train Ride _____

2. Draw the hands on the clock to show the time for the Dolphin Show.

3. The class left school 30 minutes before they got to the Bird House.

   Draw the hands and write the time on the clocks to show what time they left school.

Topic 13 | Performance Assessment

seven hundred thirty-nine 739

4. The class will see the Small Animals for 30 minutes.

What time will it be then? Choose a way to show the time.

[ ]

The class will be back at school 30 minutes after they finish seeing the Small Animals.

What time will it be then? Choose a way to show the time.

[ ]

5. Carol says that this clock shows the same time that Lunch starts.

Do you agree with her?

Circle **Yes** or **No**.

Explain your answer.

_____
_____
_____
_____
_____

TOPIC 14: Reason with Shapes and Their Attributes

Essential Question: How can you define shapes and compose new shapes?

Digital Resources: Solve, Learn, Glossary, Tools, Assessment, Help, Games

Materials can be made into shapes that help do a job.

Bricks are rectangular prisms. They stack to make buildings!

Wow! Let's do this project and learn more.

Math and Science Project: Use Shapes to Build

Find Out Talk to friends and relatives about everyday objects that have special shapes. Discuss how the shape is important for its use.

Journal: Make a Book Show what you found out. In your book, also:
- Draw different buildings using circles, squares, rectangles, cylinders, and rectangular prisms.
- In your drawings, show how shapes can be put together to make new shapes.

Topic 14   seven hundred forty-one   741

Name _____

Review What You Know

Vocabulary

1. Scott **sorted** these shapes. Put an X on the one that does not belong.

2. Circle the object that is a **different** shape.

3. Circle the **square**.

Same and Different

4. Draw a shape that is the same as the one below.

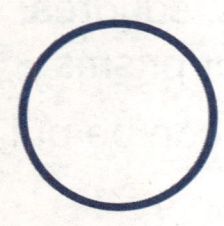

5. Draw a shape that is different from the one below.

Count by 1s

6. Write the missing numbers.

1, ____, 3, 4, ____

742 seven hundred forty-two

Topic 14

My Word Cards — Study the words on the front of the card. Complete the activity on the back.

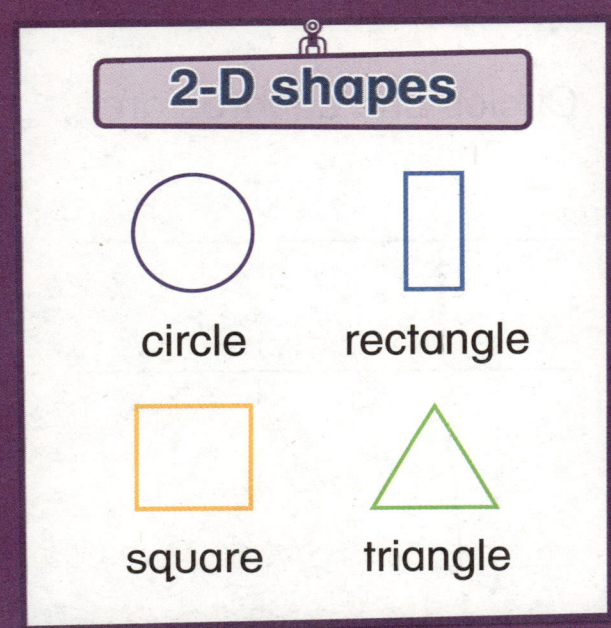

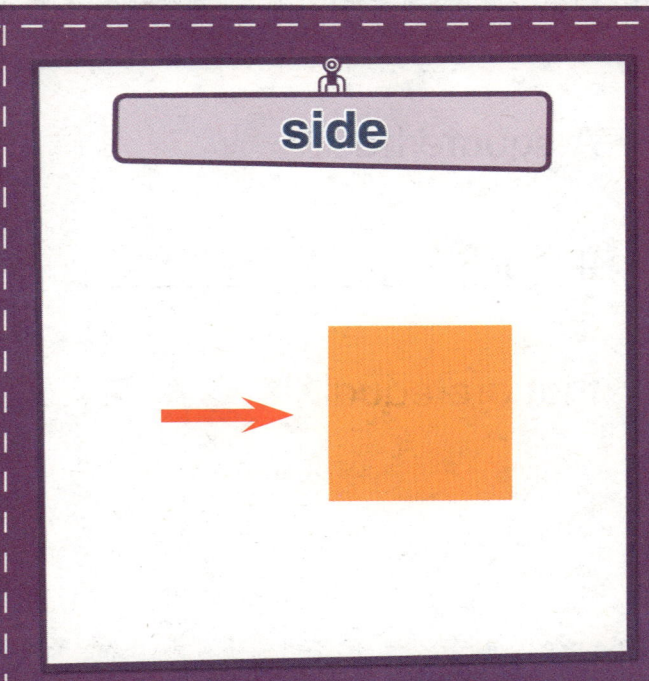

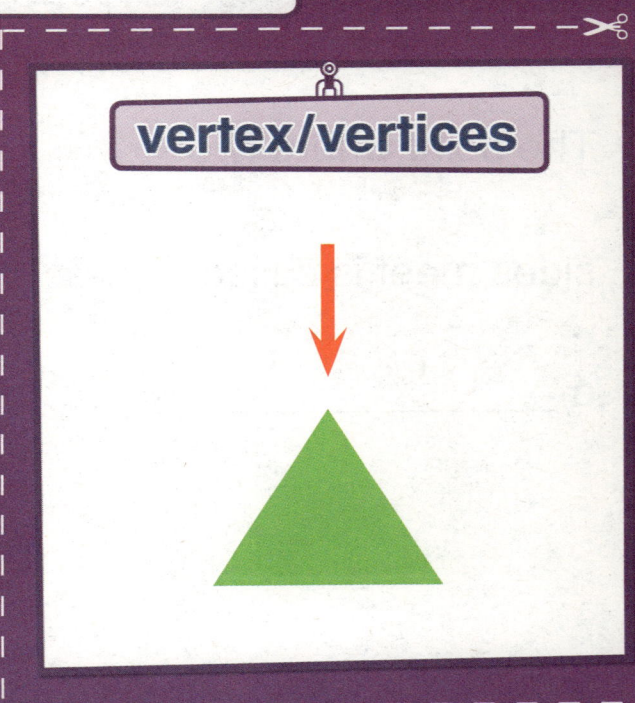

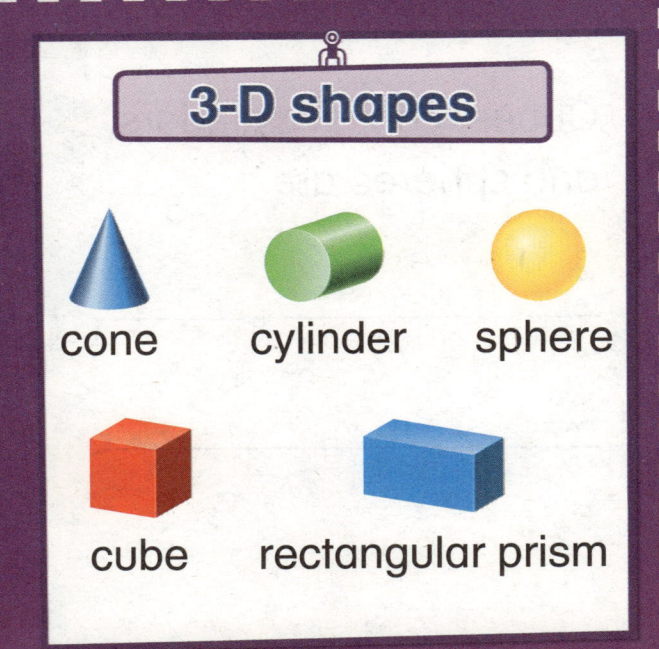

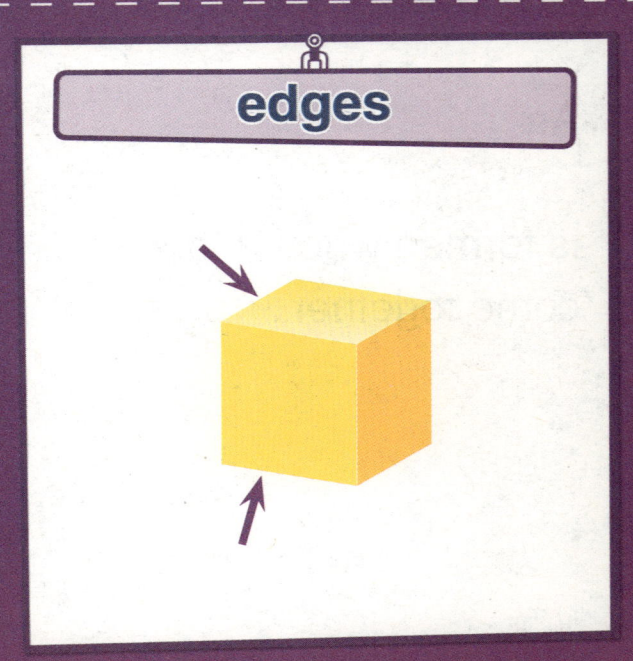

2-D shapes
- circle
- rectangle
- square
- triangle

side

vertex/vertices

3-D shapes
- cone
- cylinder
- sphere
- cube
- rectangular prism

flat surfaces

edges

Topic 14 | My Word Cards

My Word Cards — Use what you know to complete the sentences. Extend learning by writing your own sentence using each word.

The point where two sides meet is called a ___verteces___.

A square has 4 ___sides___ that are equal.

Circles and squares are ___2d___.

An ___edge___ is formed when 2 faces come together.

A cylinder has 2 ___flat surfaces___.

Cubes, cones, cylinders, and spheres are ___3d___.

My Word Cards

Study the words on the front of the card. Complete the activity on the back.

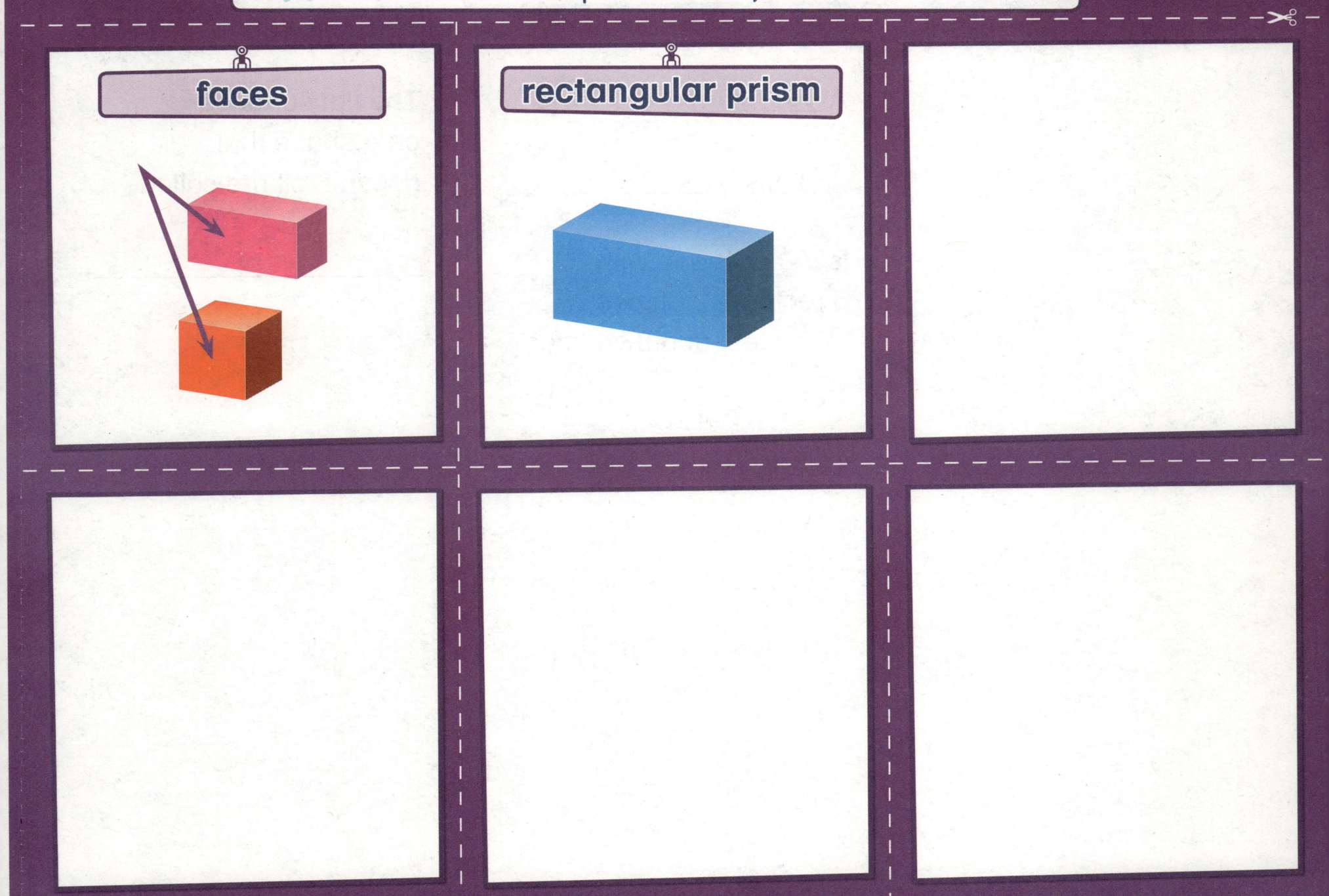

faces

rectangular prism

Topic 14 | My Word Cards

seven hundred forty-five **745**

My Word Cards

Use what you know to complete the sentences. Extend learning by writing your own sentence using each word.

A <u>rectangular prism</u> is a 3-D shape with 6 rectangular faces, 12 edges, and 8 vertices.

The flat surfaces on a shape that doesn't roll are called <u>faces</u>.

Name _____

Lesson 14-1
Use Attributes to Define Two-Dimensional (2-D) Shapes

Solve & Share

Draw an object from your classroom that matches each shape below.

How do you know that the shape you drew is the same as the one on the page?

I can ... use attributes to match shapes.

I can also look for patterns.

Square

Circle

Triangle

Rectangle

Hexagon

Topic 14 | Lesson 1   Digital Resources at SavvasRealize.com   seven hundred forty-seven **747**

triangle   circle   rectangle   square

Two-dimensional, or **2-D shapes**, are plane shapes. You can define 2-D shapes by how they look.

Some 2-D shapes have straight **sides** and some 2-D shapes do not.

3 straight sides

0 straight sides

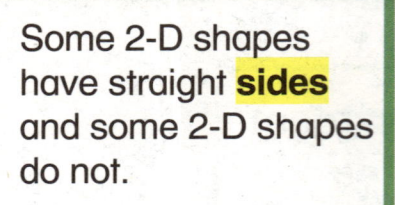

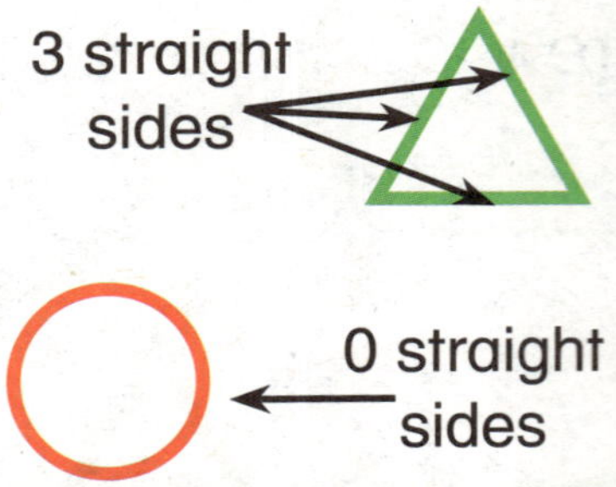

Some 2-D shapes have corners called **vertices** and some 2-D shapes do not.

3 vertices

0 vertices

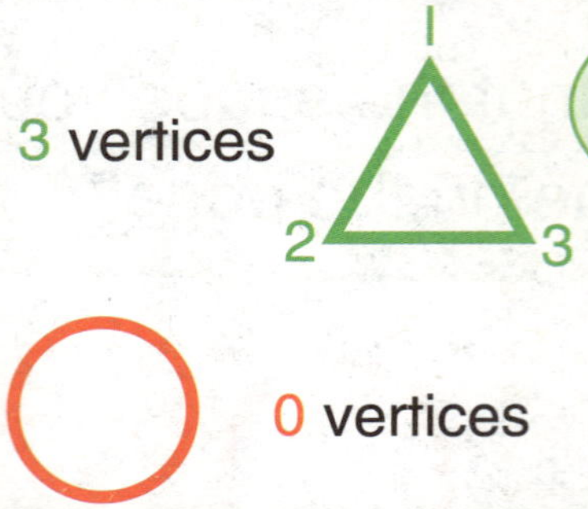

2-D shapes are closed. Their sides are all connected.

This is not a triangle. It is not a closed shape with 3 sides.

Do You Understand?

Show Me! Look at the green triangle above. How would you define it by how it looks?

Guided Practice

For each shape, tell how many straight sides or vertices, and if it is closed or not.

1.  How many straight sides? 4
   Closed? Yes

2.  How many vertices? ____
   Closed? ____

3.  How many straight sides? ____
   Closed? ____

748   seven hundred forty-eight   Topic 14 | Lesson 1

Name _____

Independent Practice Draw each shape.

4. Draw a closed shape with 3 vertices.

5. Draw a closed shape with 0 straight sides.

6. Draw a closed shape with more than 3 vertices.

7. Circle the closed shapes.

8. **Higher Order Thinking** Look at the shapes in each group. Explain how the shapes are sorted.

Group 1   **Group 2**

_____

_____

_____

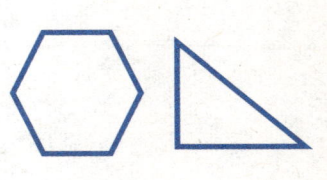

Topic 14 | Lesson 1

Problem Solving Solve each problem below.

9. Be Precise Circle 3 shapes that have the same number of vertices and sides.

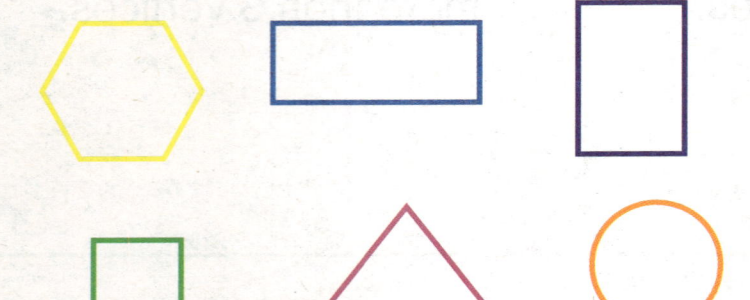

10. Be Precise Circle 3 shapes that do **NOT** have any vertices.

11. Higher Order Thinking Think about a 2-D shape. Write a riddle about the shape for a partner to solve.

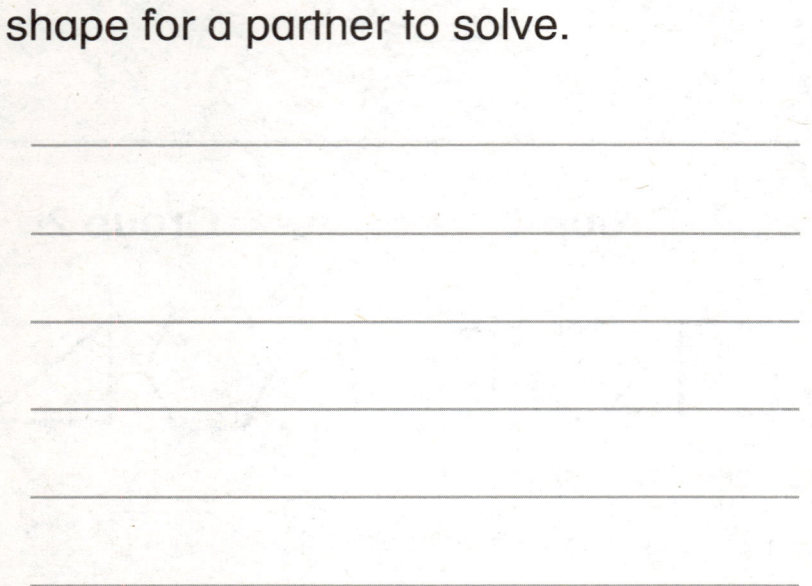

12. Assessment I have 4 vertices. My sides are equal. Which shape or shapes can I **NOT** be? Choose all that apply.

750 seven hundred fifty Topic 14 | Lesson 1

Name _____

Homework & Practice 14-1
Use Attributes to Define Two-Dimensional (2-D) Shapes

Another Look! You can sort shapes by the number of straight sides and vertices. A shape is closed if the sides are connected.

Tell if the shape is closed or not. Then count the straight sides and vertices.

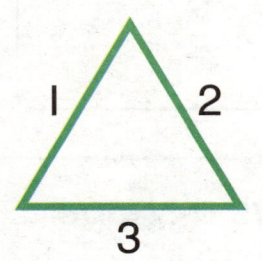

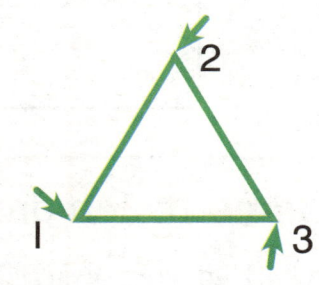

A triangle is a closed shape with 3 straight sides and 3 vertices.

Closed? **Yes** A square has **4** straight sides and **4** vertices.

HOME ACTIVITY Draw a square, a rectangle, a triangle, and a circle. Have your child tell how many straight sides and how many vertices each shape has.

For each shape, tell if it is closed or not. Then tell how many sides and vertices it has.

1. Closed? ____ A circle has ____ straight sides and ____ vertices.

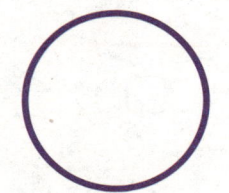

2. Closed? ____ A rectangle has ____ straight sides and ____ vertices.

3. Closed? ____ A hexagon has ____ straight sides and ____ vertices.

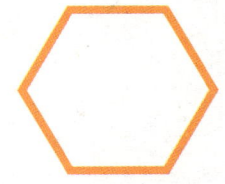

Topic 14 | Lesson 1 Digital Resources at SavvasRealize.com seven hundred fifty-one 751

Draw each shape.

4. Draw a shape with more than 3 sides.

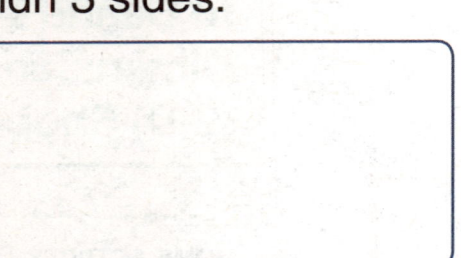

5. Draw a shape with 4 vertices.

6. Draw a shape with no vertices.

7. Higher Order Thinking A rhombus is a closed shape with 4 equal sides and 4 vertices. Circle the shape that is not a rhombus. Explain how you know.

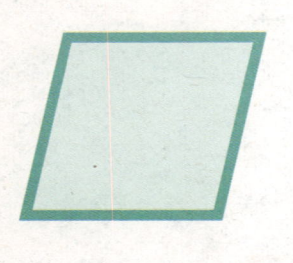

8. Assessment Jen draws a shape with 4 sides and 4 vertices. Which could be Jen's shape? Choose all that apply.

752 seven hundred fifty-two   Topic 14 | Lesson 1

Name _____

Solve & Share

Are all these figures the same kind of shape? Explain how you know.

Lesson 14-2
Defining and Non-Defining Attributes of 2-D Shapes

I can ...
define 2-D shapes by their attributes.

I can also make math arguments.

Topic 14 | Lesson 2

seven hundred fifty-three **753**

Are these all the same kind of shape?

Shapes are defined by the number of straight sides and vertices, and whether they are closed or not.

This is a closed shape. It has 4 vertices and 2 pairs of sides that are the same length. This shape is a rectangle.

Shapes are not defined by color.

These shapes are all blue. But I see a rectangle, a circle, and a hexagon.

Shapes are not defined by size or position.

These are all rectangles!

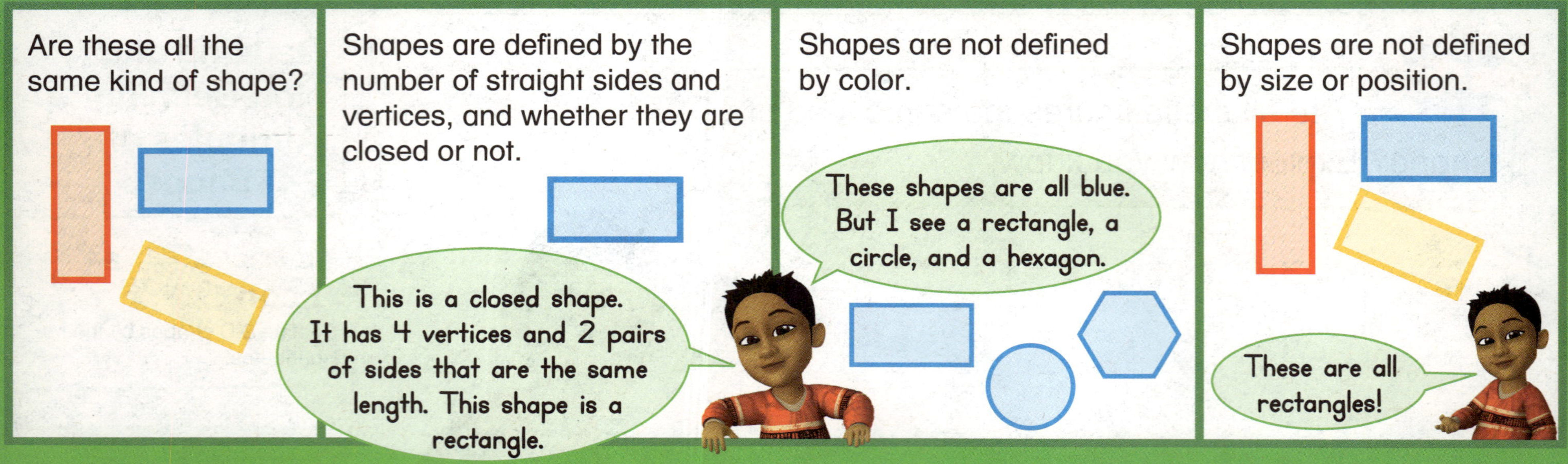

Do You Understand?

Show Me! Draw 4 hexagons. How do you know they are all hexagons?

Guided Practice

Circle the words that are true for the shape.

1.  All squares:

   are blue.

   have 4 equal sides.

   are closed shapes.

   are small.

Name _____

Independent Practice

Circle the words that are true for each shape.

2. All triangles:

    have 3 sides.

    have 3 equal sides.

    are tall.

    are orange.

3. All circles:

    are blue.

    have 0 vertices.

    are small.

    have 0 straight sides.

4. **Higher Order Thinking** Tim says that this is a triangle. Is he correct? Tell why or why not.

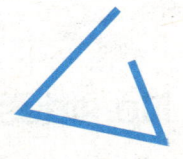

Topic 14 | Lesson 2

seven hundred fifty-five **755**

Problem Solving Solve each problem below.

5. Use Tools Do all triangles have equal sides? Circle **Yes** or **No**.

Yes   No

Choose a tool to show how you know.

6. Higher Order Thinking Jake says both of these shapes are hexagons because they are closed, have 6 straight sides, and are red. Do you agree? Explain.

7. Assessment Match each shape with the words that describe it.

Rectangle   Circle   Triangle

3 vertices   4 vertices   No sides or vertices

Name _____

Homework & Practice 14-2

Defining and Non-Defining Attributes of 2-D Shapes

Another Look! You can use certain features to identify shapes.

How can you tell if a shape is a square?

"These shapes are all blue. They also all have 4 sides. But only some of them are squares."

"These shapes are all different colors and sizes. But they are all squares."

All squares:
- have 4 equal sides.
- are blue.
- are small.
- have 4 vertices.

HOME ACTIVITY Work with your child to find shapes around the house (such as triangles, squares, and hexagons). Then make lists of defining attributes for each shape. Ask him or her to draw or construct 3 different examples of each shape.

Circle the words that are true for the shape.

1.  All triangles:
   - are yellow.
   - are short.
   - have 3 straight sides.
   - have 3 vertices.

Topic 14 | Lesson 2

Digital Resources at SavvasRealize.com

seven hundred fifty-seven **757**

Circle the words that are true for the shape.

2. 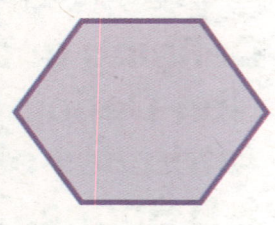 All hexagons: are purple.   have 6 equal sides.

have 6 straight sides.   have 6 vertices.

3. **Higher Order Thinking** Danielle says these shapes are rectangles because they are both tall shapes with 4 straight sides and 4 vertices. Do you agree? Why or why not? What other shapes have 4 straight sides and 4 vertices?

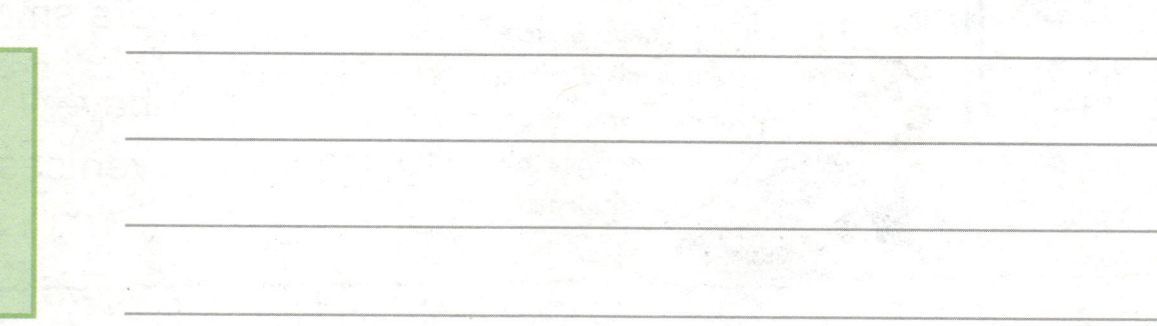

_____

_____

_____

4. ✓**Assessment** Match each shape with the words that describe it.

Triangle   Square   Hexagon   Circle

4 equal sides   3 vertices   6 sides   No sides or vertices

Name _____

Solve & Share

Use the items your teacher gave you to make 2 different rectangles. Tell what makes each shape a rectangle.

Lesson 14-3
Build and Draw 2-D Shapes by Attributes

I can ...
use different materials to make shapes.

I can also use math tools correctly.

Rectangle 1   **Rectangle 2**

Topic 14 | Lesson 3 — seven hundred fifty-nine **759**

2-D shapes can be made using all kinds of materials.

You have to think about how your shape looks.

I am going to make a triangle. What makes a triangle a triangle?

A triangle has 3 sides and 3 vertices.

This is a triangle, too.

It looks a little different but the shape still has 3 sides and 3 vertices.

Do You Understand?

Show Me! Sue made the shape on the right. Is it also a hexagon? Tell how you know.

Guided Practice Make a square. Use materials your teacher gives you. Glue or tape the square in the box. Explain how you know it is a square.

1.

760 seven hundred sixty

Topic 14 | Lesson 3

Name _____

Independent Practice Use materials your teacher gives you to make each shape. Glue or tape the shape in the box. Explain how you know the shape is correct.

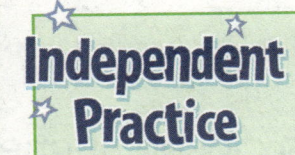

2. Make a circle.

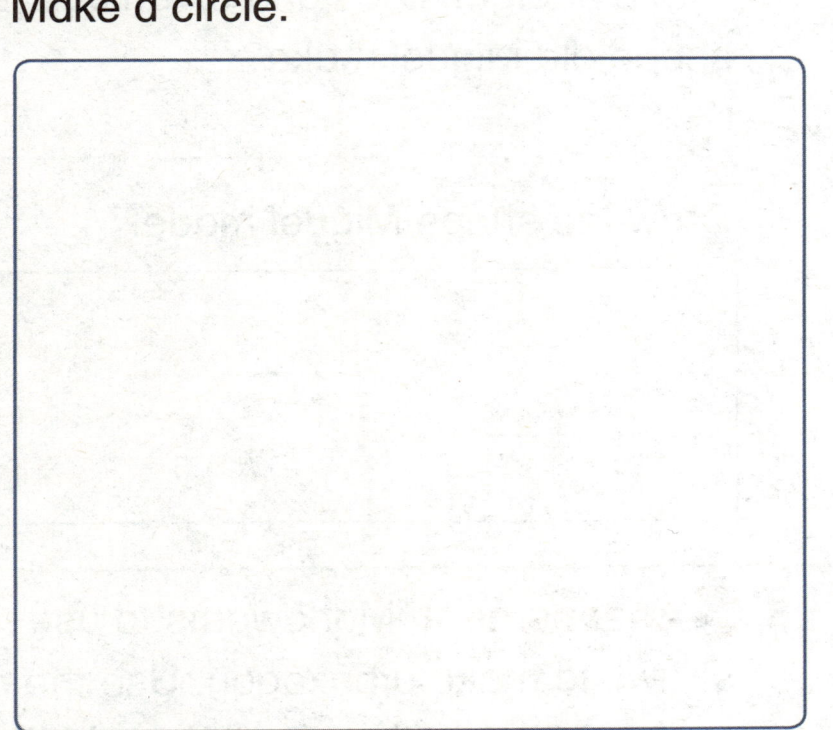

3. Make a rectangle.

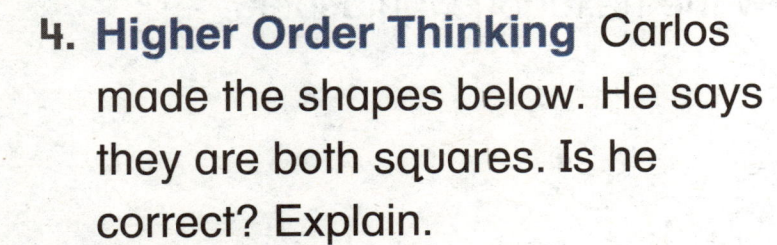

4. Higher Order Thinking Carlos made the shapes below. He says they are both squares. Is he correct? Explain.

_____
_____
_____
_____

Topic 14 | Lesson 3

seven hundred sixty-one **761**

Problem Solving Draw a picture to solve each problem below. Use pattern blocks to help you.

5. **Reasoning** Sandy makes a closed shape with 4 equal sides. What shape did she make?

   _____

   Draw the shape Sandy made.

6. **Reasoning** Miguel makes a closed shape with 3 straight sides and 3 vertices. What shape did Miguel make?

   _____

   Draw the shape Miguel made.

7. **Higher Order Thinking** Use a piece of paper to make a square. Then turn the square into a triangle. What did you do? Explain.

8. **Assessment** Mark wants to use straws to make a hexagon. Use the dots to draw straight lines that show Mark how the hexagon would look.

762 seven hundred sixty-two Topic 14 | Lesson 3

Name _____

Homework & Practice 14-3
Build and Draw 2-D Shapes by Attributes

Another Look! You can use different materials to make shapes.

This circle was made with string.

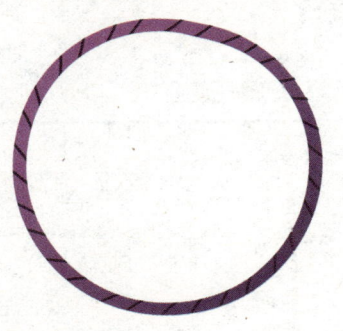

A circle has 0 sides and 0 vertices.

This _rectangle_ was made with craft sticks.

The opposite sides of a _rectangle_ are equal.

HOME ACTIVITY Have your child use materials you have at home to make different shapes. Have him or her count the number of sides for each shape.

Use materials to make each shape. Glue or tape the shape in the box.

1. Make a triangle. Tell 1 thing about a triangle.

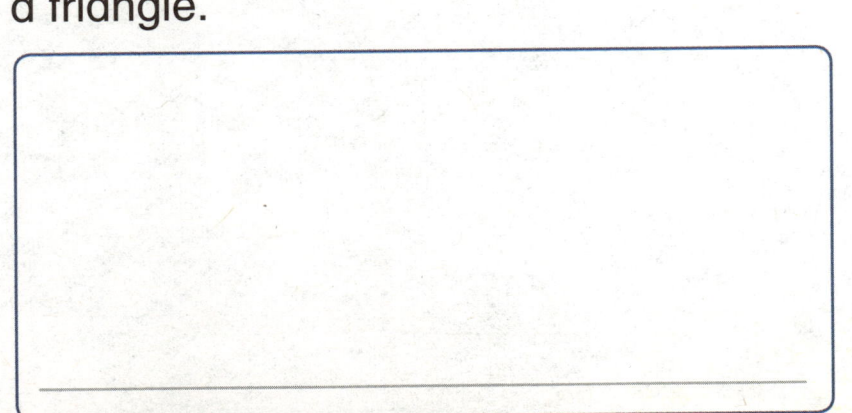

2. Make a square. Tell 1 thing about a square.

Topic 14 | Lesson 3 · Digital Resources at SavvasRealize.com · seven hundred sixty-three **763**

Draw a picture to solve each problem below.

3. Lucia made a shape. The shape has 4 sides. The shape has opposite sides that are equal. What shape did Lucia make?

Lucia made a _____.

4. Yani made a shape. The shape has no sides. The shape has no vertices. What shape did Yani make?

Yani made a _____.

5. **Higher Order Thinking** Use shapes to draw a house. Label each shape you used.

6. **Assessment** Lee made a triangle using toothpicks. He knows that a triangle has 3 sides, but does not know how many vertices it has. Circle each vertex on the triangle below.

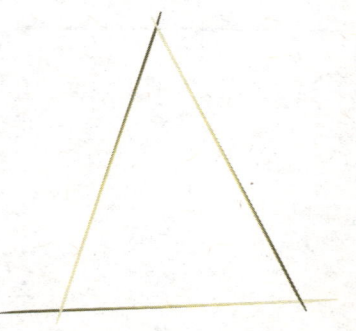

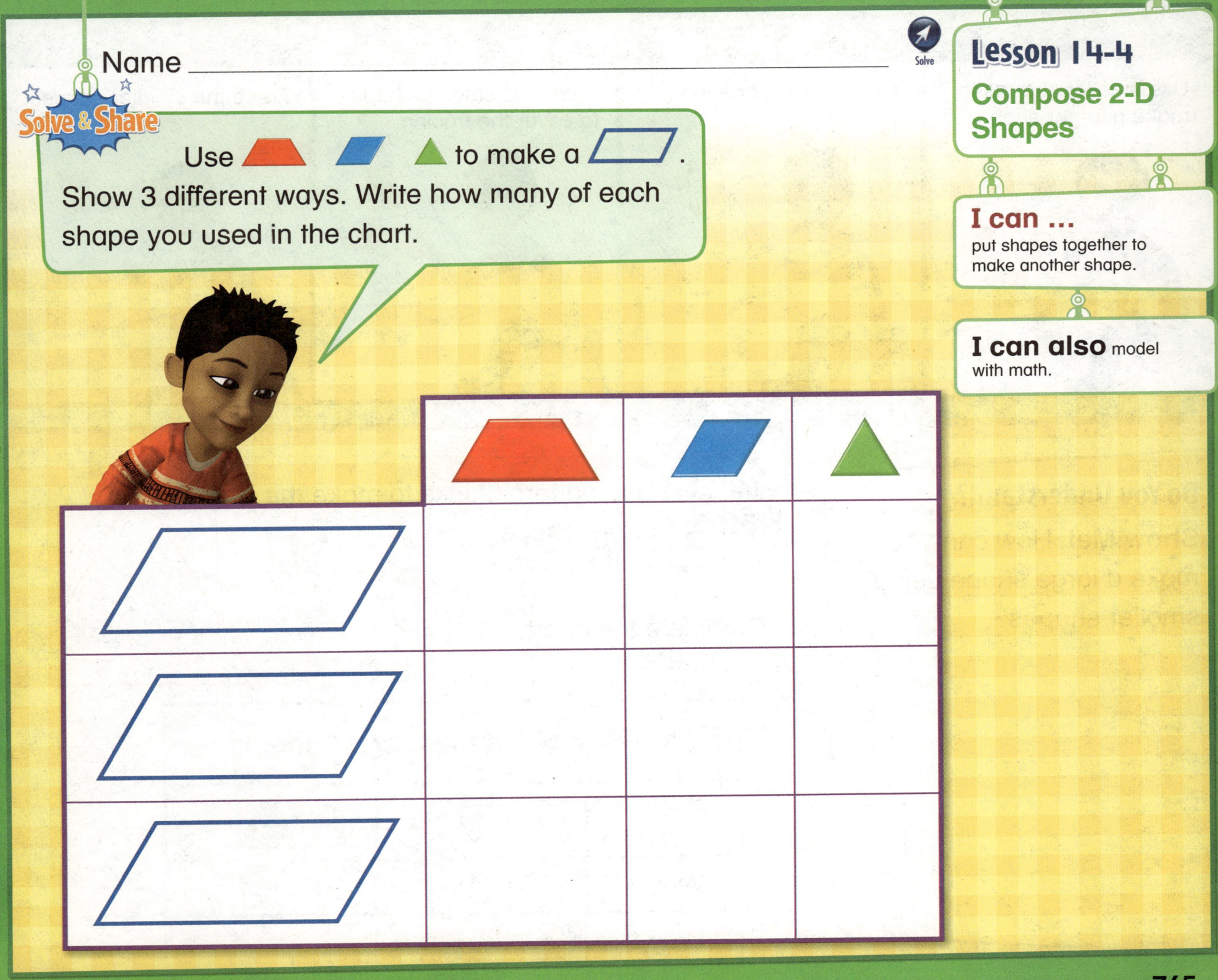

Name _____

Solve & Share

Use 🟥 🔷 🔺 to make a ▱.
Show 3 different ways. Write how many of each shape you used in the chart.

Lesson 14-4
Compose 2-D Shapes

I can ...
put shapes together to make another shape.

I can also model with math.

Topic 14 | Lesson 4 seven hundred sixty-five **765**

Use smaller shapes to make a larger shape.

Trace the larger shape.

Then use smaller shapes to cover the tracing.

Trace the smaller shapes.

Do You Understand?

Show Me! How can you make a large shape using smaller shapes?

☆ **Guided Practice** ☆ Use pattern blocks to make the larger shape.

1. Complete the chart.

Ways to Make the Large Triangle

Shapes I Used	▱	▲
Way 1	0	4
Way 2		

766 seven hundred sixty-six

Topic 14 | Lesson 4

Name _____

Independent Practice
Use the smaller shapes to make larger shapes.

2. Complete the chart to show a list of ways you can make the hexagon. Use pattern blocks to help.

Ways to Make

Shapes I Used	🟥	🟦	🔺
Way 1			
Way 2			
Way 3			

3. Use 🟢 to make a 🟡.

Draw the 🟢 in the space below.

4. **Higher Order Thinking** Use 3 pattern blocks to make a new shape. Trace the pattern blocks. What shapes did you use? What shape did you make?

Topic 14 | Lesson 4

seven hundred sixty-seven 767

Problem Solving Use smaller shapes to make bigger shapes.

5. **Make Sense** Two of which shape can make ⬤ ?

6. **Make Sense** Two of which shape can make ⬢ ?

7. **Higher Order Thinking** Name and draw the shape you will make if you put the orange pattern blocks together with their full sides touching. Explain how you know.

8. **Assessment** Nicole wants to make a hexagon. She has 1 ◢. Which set of shapes could she use to complete the hexagon?

Ⓐ
Ⓒ
Ⓑ
Ⓓ

768 seven hundred sixty-eight

Topic 14 | Lesson 4

Name _____

Homework & Practice 14-4
Compose 2-D Shapes

Another Look! You can put shapes together to make new shapes.

You can make a 🟡 using 3 🔷.

You can make a 🟥 using 3 △.

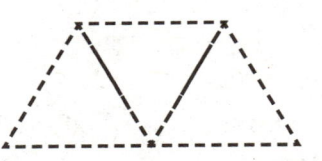

HOME ACTIVITY Have your child cut out triangles, squares, and rectangles from old newspapers and magazines. Have him or her use the shapes to make new shapes.

Circle the shapes you can use to make each shape.

1. Make a 🟧.

2. Make a 🟥.

Topic 14 | Lesson 4 — seven hundred sixty-nine 769

Solve each problem below.

3. **Number Sense** Write the number of each shape needed to make ⬡.

   ___ ▲   ___ ▭   ___ ◆

4. Kerry uses these shapes to make a new shape.

   Circle the shape Kerry makes.

5. Tony uses these shapes to make a new shape.

   Circle the shape Tony makes.

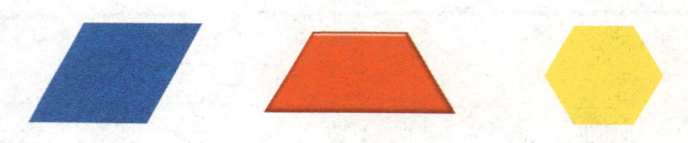

6. **Higher Order Thinking** Carlos wants to use 3 ▲ to make a square. Can he? Explain.

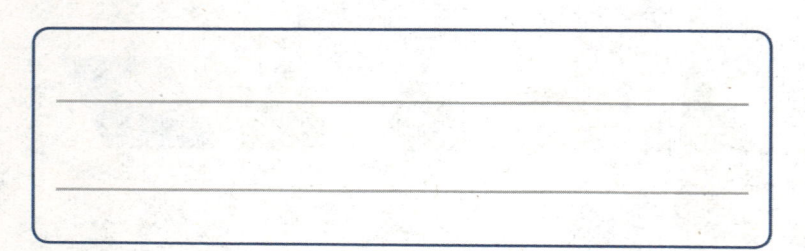

7. **Assessment** How many ◆ does Adam need to make a ⬡?

   1   2   3   4
   Ⓐ   Ⓑ   Ⓒ   Ⓓ

Name _____

Solve & Share

Use your shapes to make a small boat. Then trace the boat in the space below.

Lesson 14-5

Compose New 2-D Shapes from 2-D Shapes

I can ...
use shapes to make different shapes.

I can also reason about math.

Topic 14 | Lesson 5

Digital Resources at SavvasRealize.com

seven hundred seventy-one **771**

You can use shapes to make pictures.

I can use a △ and a ☐ to make a house!

Add shapes to change the picture.

I can make a larger house! I can add a ◇ and 1 more ☐.

I can make the house even larger! I can add 2 more ☐.

Here are more pictures you can make.

Do You Understand?

Show Me! How do you use shapes to make a picture?

Guided Practice

Start with a triangle and use pattern blocks to make a picture. Trace around your shapes to show your picture. Write how many of each shape you used.

1.

772 seven hundred seventy-two

Topic 14 | Lesson 5

Name _____

Independent Practice

Use any of the pattern blocks shown to make pictures. Trace around your shapes to show your pictures. Write how many of each shape you used for each picture.

2.

____ △   ____ ◻   ____ ⬟   ____ ◊

3.

____ △   ____ ⬟   ____ ╱╱   ____ ⬡

Topic 14 | Lesson 5

seven hundred seventy-three **773**

Problem Solving Solve the problems below.

4. **Model** Dana started making a flower using these pattern blocks. Draw more leaves and petals to help her finish.

5. **Higher Order Thinking** Use pattern blocks to make a picture of a fish.

6. **Assessment** Jeff is making a model of this arrow. Which shape does he need to add to his model to finish it?

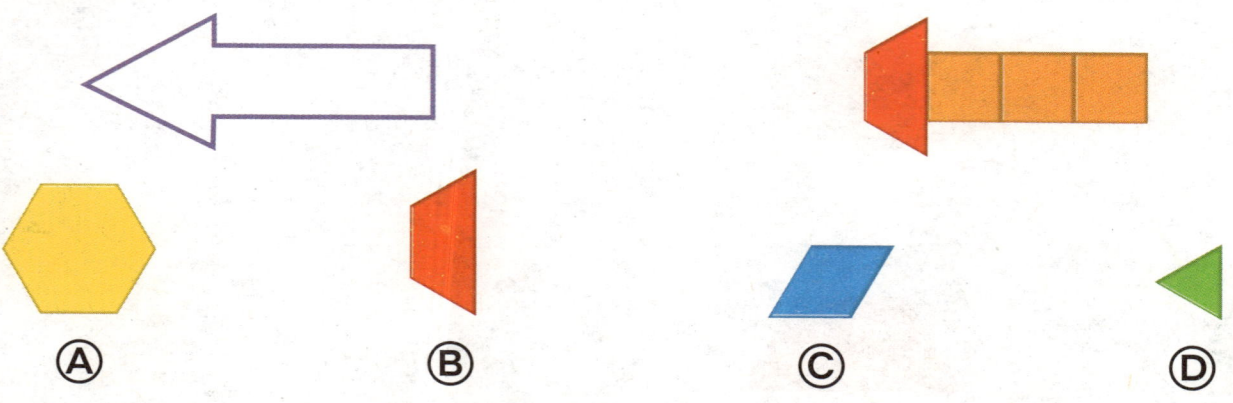

Ⓐ   Ⓑ   Ⓒ   Ⓓ

774 seven hundred seventy-four

Copyright © Savvas Learning Company LLC. All Rights Reserved.

Topic 14 | Lesson 5

Name _____

Homework & Practice 14-5
Compose New 2-D Shapes from 2-D Shapes

Another Look! You can use different blocks to make the same picture.

Finish the apple by tracing blocks that make a hexagon without using the hexagon block.

Which shapes did you use? __2__

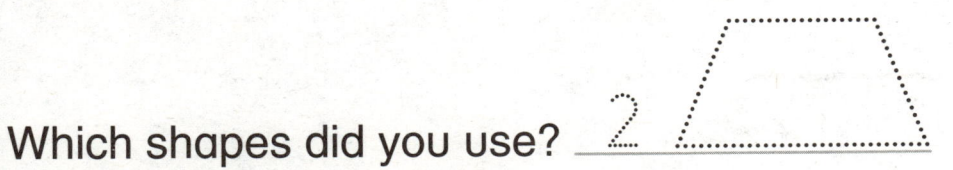

HOME ACTIVITY Ask your child to cut out 2-D shapes such as rectangles, squares, circles, and triangles. Have him or her put the shapes together to make a picture.

1. Finish the turtle without using triangles.

Solve the problems below.

2. **Reasoning** Write the number of each block used to make this microphone.

   How many triangles? _____   How many squares? _____

   How many trapezoids? _____   How many rhombuses? _____

3. **Higher Order Thinking** What are two different ways to fill in this alligator? Draw or explain how you know.

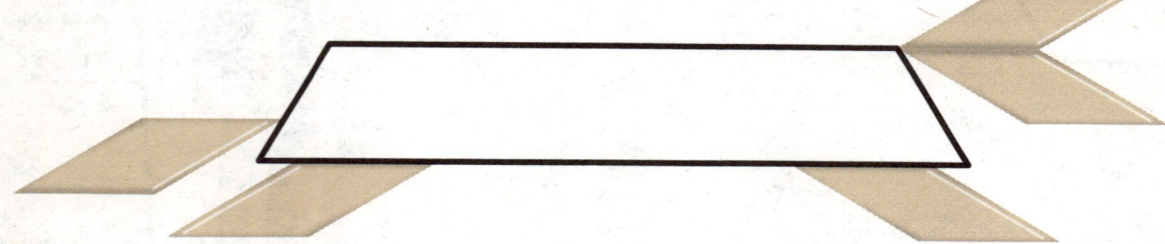

   Way 1: _____

   Way 2: _____

4. **Assessment** José is making a picture of a bunny. He is missing the matching ear. Which block is missing?

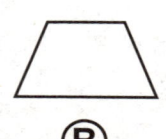

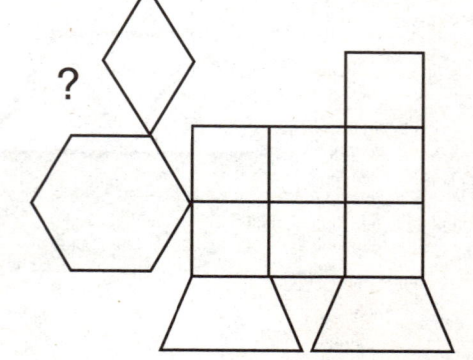

   Ⓐ   Ⓑ   Ⓒ   Ⓓ

Name _____

Lesson 14-6
Use Attributes to Define Three-Dimensional (3-D) Shapes

Solve & Share

Can you find objects in the classroom that are shaped like the objects below? Write the name of each object you find.

I can ...
define 3-D shapes by their number of edges, vertices, and faces or flat surfaces.

I can also reason about math.

cube

sphere

rectangular prism

cone

cylinder

Topic 14 | Lesson 6   Digital Resources at SavvasRealize.com   seven hundred seventy-seven **777**

Three-dimensional (3-D) shapes can be grouped in different ways.

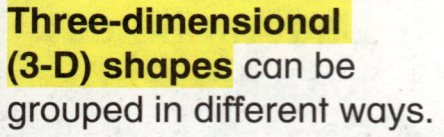

A cylinder has 2 flat surfaces. A cone only has 1.

The **flat surface** of each of these shapes is a circle.

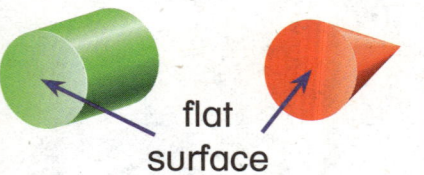

flat surface

These shapes have **edges** and vertices. Their flat surfaces are called **faces**.

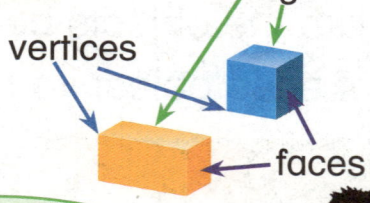

edges
vertices
faces

The faces of the cube and the **rectangular prism** are all rectangles.

A sphere is a 3-D shape that has no flat surfaces, no edges, and no vertices.

Do You Understand?
Show Me! Do 3-D shapes always have either faces, flat surfaces, or vertices? Explain.

Guided Practice
Write how many faces or flat surfaces and vertices each 3-D shape has.

	3-D shape	Number of faces or flat surfaces	Number of vertices	Number of edges
1.		6	8	12
2.		1	1	0

778 seven hundred seventy-eight

Topic 14 | Lesson 6

Name _____

Independent Practice
Write how many faces or flat surfaces and vertices each object has.

Object	Number of faces or flat surfaces	Number of vertices	Number of edges
3. (soccer ball)	0	0	0
4. (cube)	6	8	10
5. (drum)	2	0	0

6. **Higher Order Thinking** Lily has an object that looks like a 3-D shape. The object has 2 flat surfaces and 0 vertices.

Draw an object that Lily could have.

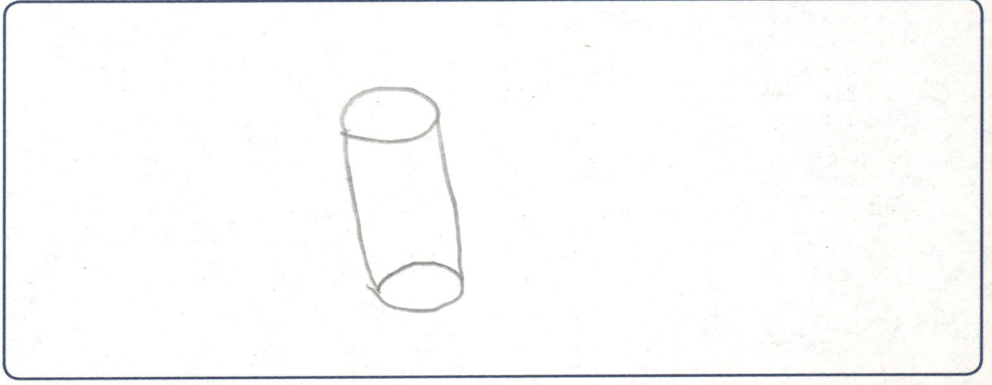

Topic 14 | Lesson 6

seven hundred seventy-nine 779

Problem Solving Solve each problem below.

7. This shape is a cone. Which shape below is also a cone? How do you know?

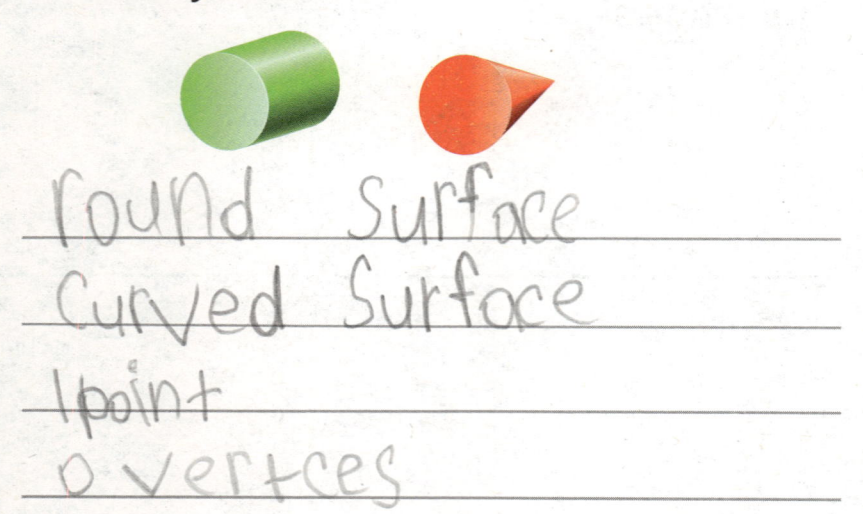

round surface
curved surface
1 point
0 vertces

8. Reasoning Nikki and Ben each buy 1 item from the store. Nikki's item has 4 more edges than vertices. Ben's item has the same number of flat surfaces and edges.

Draw a circle around Nikki's item. Draw a box around Ben's item.

9. Higher Order Thinking Draw and label a 3-D shape. Then write a sentence describing your 3-D shape.

It has 6 faces

10. Assessment I have 6 faces. I have 8 vertices. Which 3-D shape could I be? Choose all that apply.

☐ sphere
☒ cube
☒ rectangular prism
☐ cylinder

Homework & Practice 14-6
Use Attributes to Define Three-Dimensional (3-D) Shapes

Another Look! Flat surfaces, faces, edges, and vertices can be used to describe 3-D shapes.

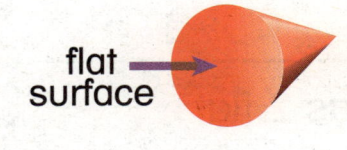

← flat surface

← vertex

A cone has 1 flat surface.

A cube has 8 vertices.

A rectangular prism has 6 faces.

A cylinder has 0 edges.

HOME ACTIVITY Gather household objects that look like the following 3-D shapes: cube, rectangular prism, sphere, cone, and cylinder. Have your child count the number of faces or flat surfaces, edges, and vertices on each shape. Then have him or her choose 2 shapes and tell how they are alike and different.

Circle the 3-D shape that answers each question.

1. Which 3-D shape has 1 flat surface and 1 vertex?

2. Which 3-D shape has 0 flat surfaces and 0 vertices?

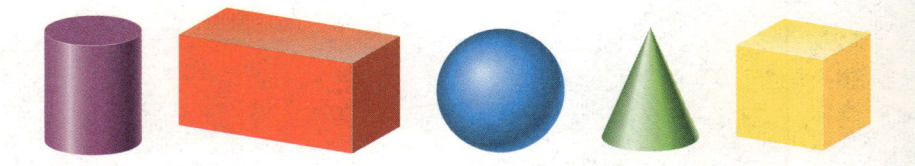

Solve the problems below.

3. **Vocabulary** Circle the number of vertices on a **rectangular prism**.

   0 vertices   4 vertices   5 vertices   8 vertices

4. Circle the shapes that have 6 faces and 12 edges.

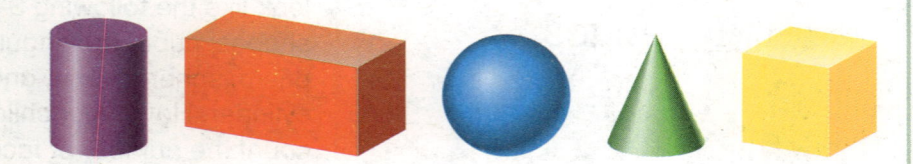

5. Circle the shape that has 2 flat surfaces and 0 vertices.

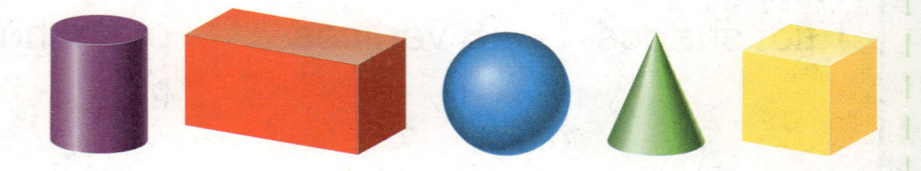

6. **Higher Order Thinking** Draw or name two 3-D shapes. Find the total number of vertices and faces or flat surfaces.

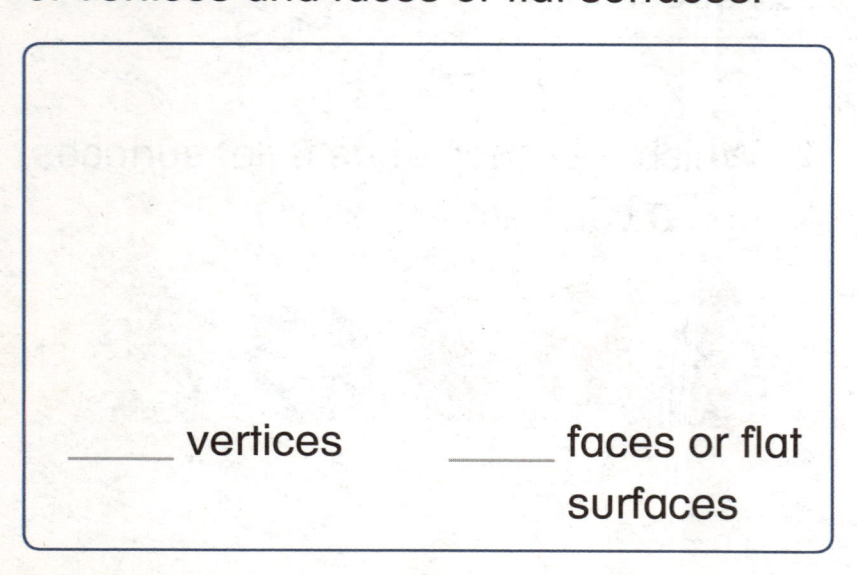

   _____ vertices   _____ faces or flat surfaces

7. **Assessment** Katie picks two of these 3-D shapes out of a bag. What is the total number of flat surfaces or faces that could be on the shapes she picked? Choose all that apply.

   ☐ 7   ☐ 10   ☐ 12   ☐ 16

782 seven hundred eighty-two

Name _____

Solve & Share

Are all three of these shapes considered cylinders? Explain why or why not.

Lesson 14-7
Defining and Non-Defining Attributes of 3-D Shapes

I can ...
choose the defining attributes of 3-D shapes.

I can also make math arguments.

Topic 14 | Lesson 7 seven hundred eighty-three **783**

Are these all the same kind of 3-D shape?

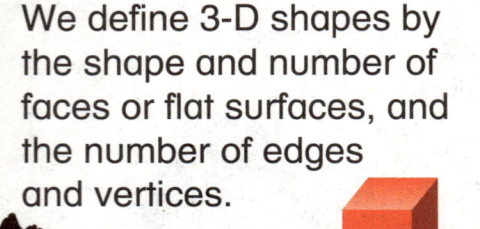

We define 3-D shapes by the shape and number of faces or flat surfaces, and the number of edges and vertices.

Just because shapes are the same size or color does not mean they are the same.

Color, size, and direction don't define a shape.

How can I define a rectangular prism?

These shapes are all green. But I see a rectangular prism, a sphere, and a cylinder.

Some things about these shapes are different, but they are all rectangular prisms!

Do You Understand?

Show Me! Write 2 things that are true about all rectangular prisms. Write 2 things that do not define rectangular prisms.

Guided Practice

Circle the words that are true for the shape.

1. All cones:

   are yellow.

   (have 1 vertex.)

   are open shapes.

   can roll.

Name _____

Independent Practice Circle the words that are true for each shape.

2. **All cubes:**

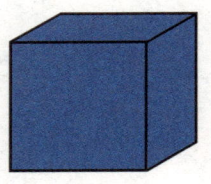

   have 12 edges.

   have 8 vertices.

   cannot roll.

   are blue.

3. **All cylinders:**

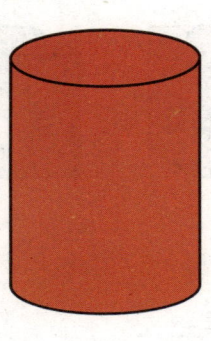

   have 2 flat surfaces.

   cannot roll.

   are red.

   can roll.

4. **Math and Science** Kevin wants to build a wall. Circle the 3-D shape or shapes he could use to build the wall.

Problem Solving* Solve the problems below.

5. Explain Do all cubes have the same number of edges?   Yes   No

Explain or draw a picture to show how you know.

6. Higher Order Thinking Steve says that both of these shapes are the same because they both have 6 faces and both are purple. Do you agree? Explain.

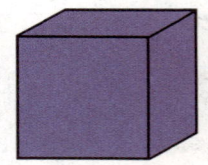

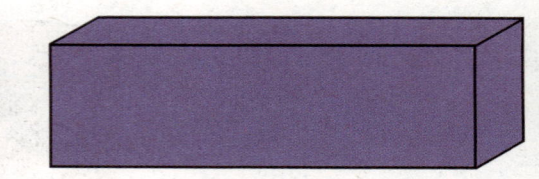

_____
_____
_____

7. Assessment Match each shape with the words that describe it.

rectangular prism   cube   sphere   cone

6 equal faces   I vertex   8 vertices   no flat surfaces or vertices

786   seven hundred eighty-six   Copyright © Savvas Learning Company LLC. All Rights Reserved.   Topic 14 | Lesson 7

Name _____

Homework & Practice 14-7

Defining and Non-Defining Attributes of 3-D Shapes

Another Look! How can you tell if a shape is a cube?

These shapes are all orange. These shapes all have 6 faces. But only some of them are cubes.

These shapes are all different colors and sizes. But they are all cubes.

So, all cubes:
- have 6 square faces.
- are orange.
- have 8 vertices.
- are large.

HOME ACTIVITY Draw or print out pictures of 3-D shapes and ask your child to tell you one attribute of each shape shown.

Circle the words that are true for the shape.

1. **All spheres:** 
   - have no flat surfaces.
   - have 3 flat surfaces.
   - cannot roll.
   - are blue.

Topic 14 | Lesson 7 — Digital Resources at SavvasRealize.com — seven hundred eighty-seven **787**

Circle the words that are true for each shape.

2. All rectangular prisms:

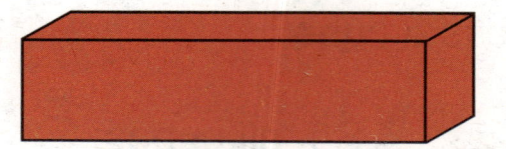

   have 6 faces.

   have 6 vertices.

   have 8 vertices.

   are red.

3. **Higher Order Thinking** Jane says that both of these shapes are cones because they both have one circular base and one vertex. Do you agree? Why or why not?

   _____

   _____

4. **Assessment** Match each shape with the trait or traits that describe it.

   cone   rectangular prism   cube   cylinder

   12 edges   0 vertices   1 vertex   8 vertices

Name _____

Lesson 14-8

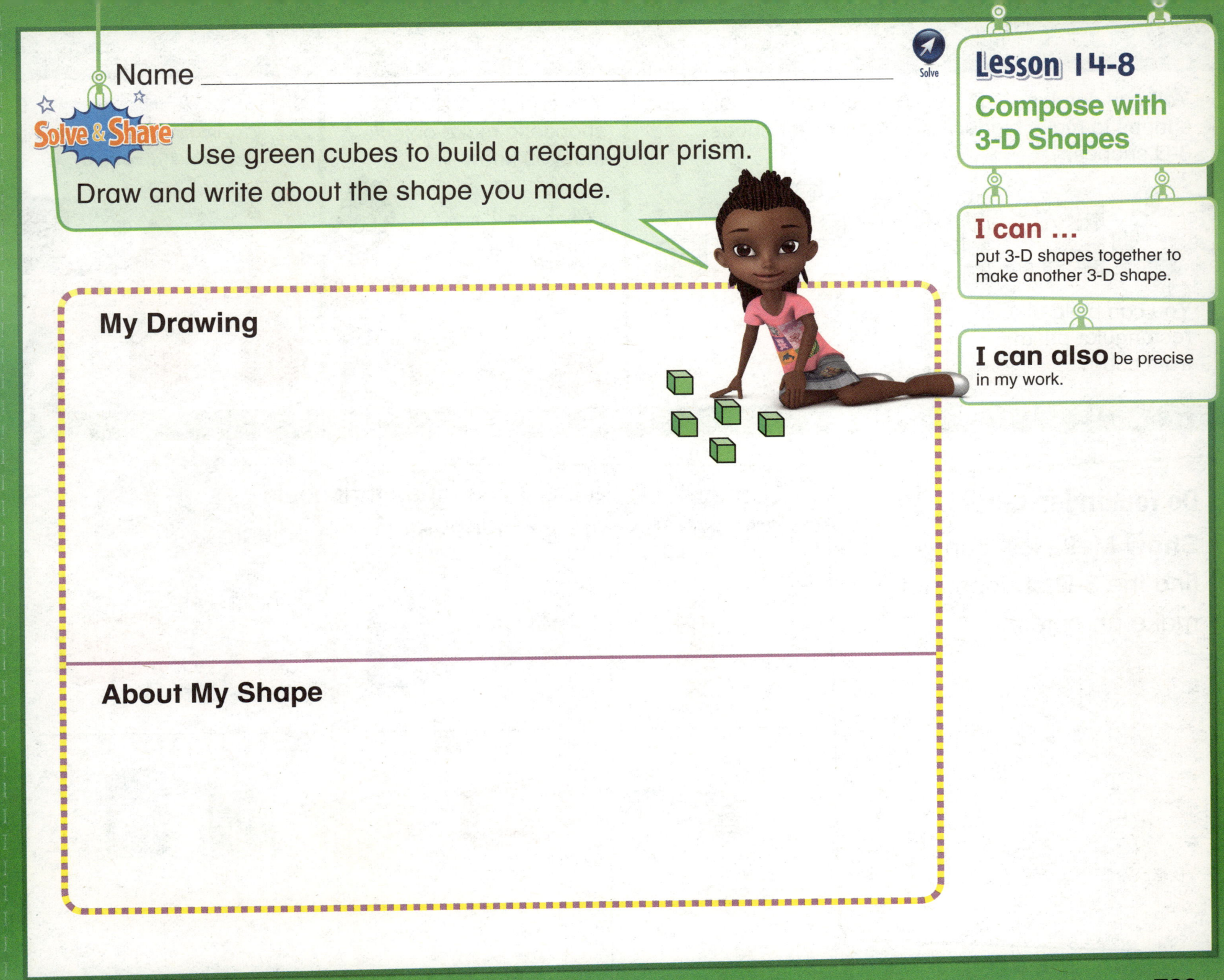

Compose with 3-D Shapes

Solve & Share

Use green cubes to build a rectangular prism. Draw and write about the shape you made.

I can ...
put 3-D shapes together to make another 3-D shape.

I can also be precise in my work.

My Drawing

About My Shape

Topic 14 | Lesson 8

You can combine 3-D shapes to make bigger 3-D shapes.

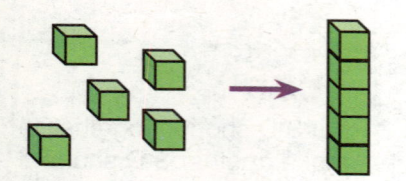

You can build a rectangular prism from cubes.

You can make a big cube from smaller cubes

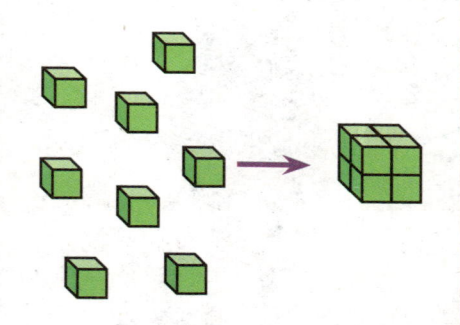

You can also use 3-D shapes to make objects that you know.

What can I make with these?

A cube, a cylinder, and a cone make a rocket!

Do You Understand?

Show Me! How can you find the 3-D shapes that make an object?

Guided Practice Circle the 3-D shapes that could be put together to make the object.

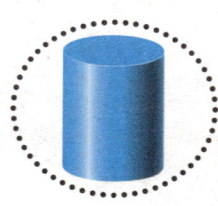

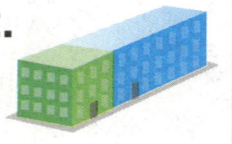

1.

2.

790 seven hundred ninety

Topic 14 | Lesson 8

Name _____

Independent Practice

Circle the 3-D shapes that could be put together to make the object.

3.

4.

5.

6. **Higher Order Thinking** Jon wants to combine 6 green cubes to make a bigger cube. Can Jon do this? Explain. Use cubes to help.

Topic 14 | Lesson 8

seven hundred ninety-one **791**

Problem Solving Solve the problems below.

7. Make Sense Ralph made this shape below with 3-D shapes.

What 3-D shapes did Ralph use?

_____

_____

8. Make Sense Kirsten has 12 ice cubes. She wants to combine the ice cubes to make an ice sculpture.

What 3-D shape could Kirsten make with the ice cubes?

_____

9. Higher Order Thinking Ellen uses two of the same shape to build a bigger 3-D shape. Her new figure has 2 flat surfaces and 0 vertices.

What 2 shapes did Ellen use?

_____

What bigger shape did Ellen build?

_____

10. Assessment Which object could be made with a △ and a ▯?

Ⓐ crayon
Ⓑ football
Ⓒ house
Ⓓ dumbbell

792 seven hundred ninety-two

Topic 14 | Lesson 8

Name _____

Homework & Practice 14-8
Compose with 3-D Shapes

Another Look! You can combine 3-D shapes to make new shapes.

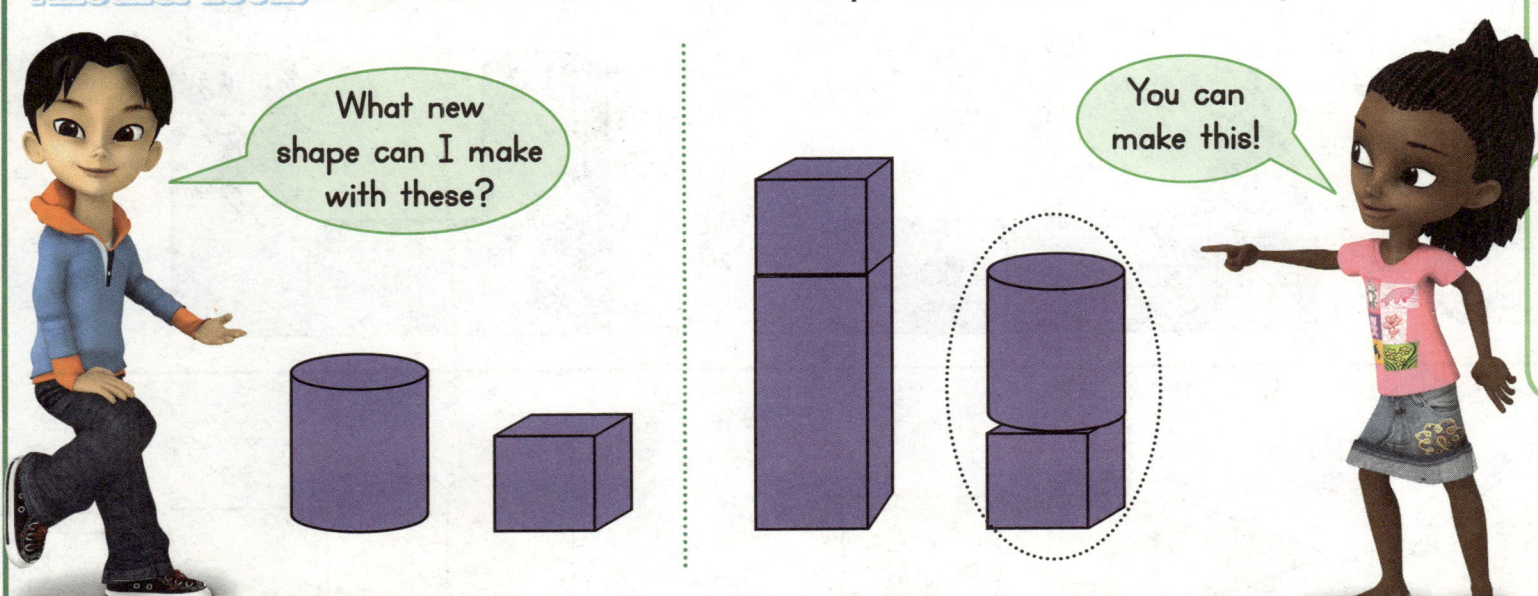

What new shape can I make with these?

You can make this!

HOME ACTIVITY Ask your child to show you how to make a new 3-D shape by using household objects such as shoe boxes, soup cans, and funnels.

Look at the two 3-D shapes. Circle the new shape you can make when combining the shapes.

1.

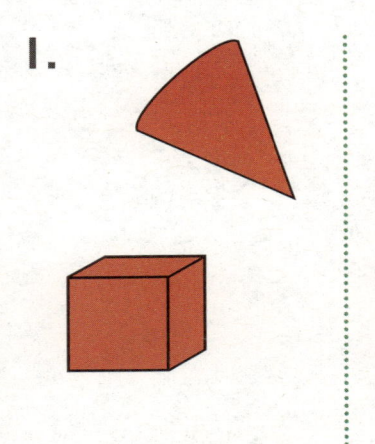

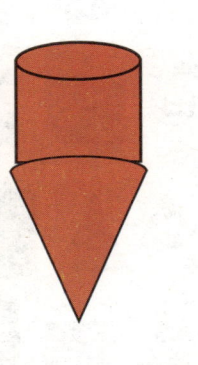

2.

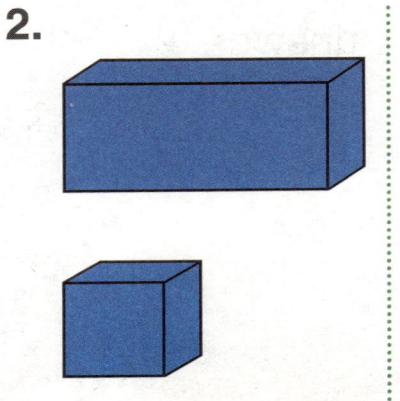

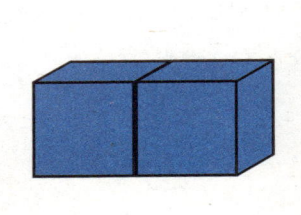

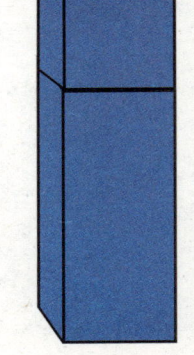

Topic 14 | Lesson 8

seven hundred ninety-three 793

The first two 3-D shapes can be used over and over to make new 3-D shapes. Circle the new shape that could be made by using the first two shapes.

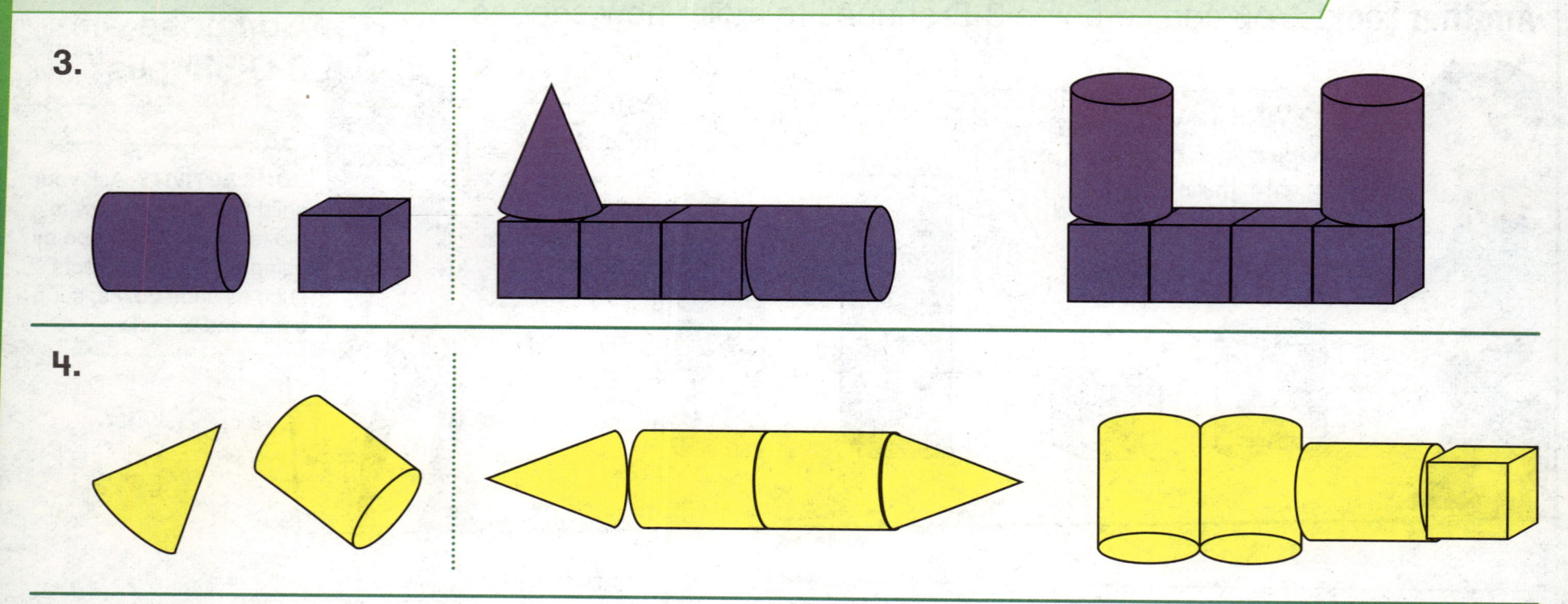

3.

4.

5. **Higher Order Thinking** Ramon wants to make a rectangular prism with 5 cubes. Can he do this? Explain. Draw cubes to show your answer.

6. **Assessment** Which shapes can make a ▭ ?

Ⓐ
Ⓑ
Ⓒ
Ⓓ

Name _____

Solve & Share

Draw an *X* on all the objects that have flat surfaces that are circles. Tell how you know the flat surfaces are circles. Make sense of the problem by circling the words that are true about the objects you crossed out.

Problem Solving

Lesson 14-9
Make Sense and Persevere

I can ...
make sense of problems.

I can also describe 2-D and 3-D shapes.

Thinking Habits
What am I asked to find?
What else can I try if I get stuck?

The objects:
- are white
- are small
- have 0 edges
- have 0 vertices
- have faces
- have flat surfaces

Topic 14 | Lesson 9

seven hundred ninety-five 795

All of these shapes are triangles. Circle the words that are true of all triangles.

What's my plan for solving the problem?

All triangles:
- have 3 sides.
- are blue.
- have a flat bottom.
- are big.
- have 3 vertices.

All triangles:
- (have 3 sides.)
- are blue.
- have a flat bottom.
- are big.
- (have 3 vertices.)

How can I make sense of the problem?

I will only circle the words that are true of all triangles.

I know triangles have 3 sides and 3 vertices.

Yes, all triangles have 3 sides and 3 vertices. I have circled the correct words.

Do You Understand?

Show Me! What words can always be used to describe a rectangular prism?

Guided Practice

Circle the words that are true of the shapes.

1. All of these shapes are squares.

All squares: are orange   are small

　　　　　　　(have 4 equal sides)   have 4 vertices

796 seven hundred ninety-six   Topic 14 | Lesson 9

Name _____

Independent Practice

Circle the words that are true of the shapes.
Then explain how you know.

2. All of these shapes are cones.

All cones: are blue   have 1 flat surface   have 1 edge   have 1 vertex

_____
_____

3. All of these shapes are hexagons.

All hexagons: are small   have 6 sides   are blue   have 6 vertices

_____
_____

Topic 14 | Lesson 9 seven hundred ninety-seven 797

Problem Solving

Performance Assessment

Arts and Crafts

Wes has cubes, spheres, cylinders, and cones. He wants to use these shapes to make art pieces for an arts and crafts sale at his school.

Wes wants to put together the right shapes for each piece of art.

4. **Be Precise** Wes wants to put together one shape that has 6 faces and one shape that has no flat surfaces. What shapes can he use? Explain.

_____

_____

_____

_____

5. **Reasoning** Wes puts two cubes together to make a new shape. Tell what shape Wes made and one thing that is true about the new shape.

_____

_____

_____

_____

Name _____

Homework & Practice 14-9
Make Sense and Persevere

Another Look! You can make sense of problems and keep working if you get stuck.

These are rectangles. Circle the words that are true of all rectangles.

All rectangles:

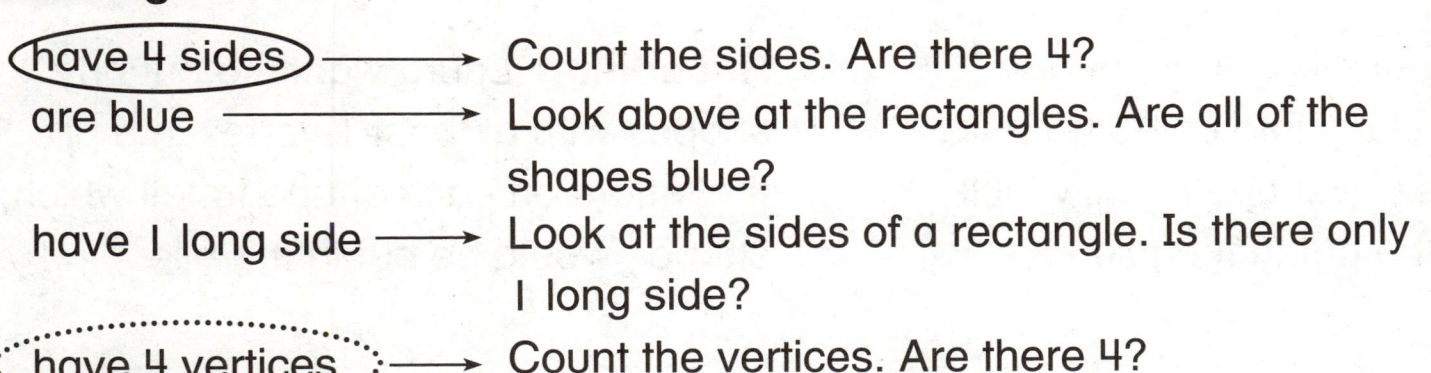

(have 4 sides) → Count the sides. Are there 4?
are blue → Look above at the rectangles. Are all of the shapes blue?
have 1 long side → Look at the sides of a rectangle. Is there only 1 long side?
(have 4 vertices) → Count the vertices. Are there 4?

HOME ACTIVITY Have your child gather examples of spheres and cubes (or any other two 2-D or 3-D combination) Ask: "What is true of all spheres (or another 2-D or 3-D shape)?" Help your child identify attributes of each shape he or she finds.

All of these shapes are rectangular prisms. Circle the words that are true of all rectangular prisms.

1. All rectangular prisms:

   are green   have 12 edges   have 4 faces   have 6 faces

Topic 14 | Lesson 9   Digital Resources at SavvasRealize.com   seven hundred ninety-nine **799**

✓ **Performance Assessment**

Puzzle Pieces

Laura is sorting her puzzle pieces into like piles. She has triangles, rectangles, squares, circles, and trapezoids. Help her sort the pieces.

A B C D E F G H I J

2. **Be Precise** Laura wants to put any shapes with 4 sides into one pile. Use the letters on each shape to tell which shapes would be put in the pile.

3. **Reasoning** Laura wants to put any shapes with at least 1 vertex in a pile. Use the letters on each shape to tell which shapes would be put in the pile.

4. **Make Sense** Sort shapes A–J into two or more piles based on similarities by drawing or writing. Then explain how you sorted.

Name _____

Show the Word

Color these sums and differences. Leave the rest white.

TOPIC 14 — **Fluency Practice Activity**

I can ...
add and subtract within 10.

| 3 | 2 | 1 |

0 + 2	5 – 3	1 + 1	10 – 7	1 + 2	0 + 3	0 + 1	10 – 9	3 – 2
6 – 4	8 – 1	8 – 6	4 – 1	6 + 4	8 – 3	6 – 5	8 + 1	5 – 5
2 + 0	2 + 2	7 – 5	3 + 0	2 + 1	6 – 3	5 – 4	9 – 8	1 + 0
4 – 2	4 + 3	9 – 7	9 – 6	4 – 4	7 + 1	2 – 1	0 + 8	4 + 5
10 – 8	2 – 0	3 – 1	7 – 4	3 + 1	2 + 8	8 – 7	4 + 0	8 – 2

The word is

_____ _____ _____

Topic 14 | Fluency Practice Activity

eight hundred one 801

TOPIC 14 Vocabulary Review

Word List
- 2-D shapes
- 3-D shapes
- edges
- faces
- flat surfaces
- rectangular prism
- side
- vertex/vertices

Understand Vocabulary

1. Circle the 2-D shape that has no vertices.

2. Circle the 2-D shape that has 4 vertices and equal sides.

3. Write what part of the shape is shown. Use the Word List.

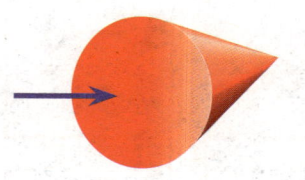

   _____

4. Write the name of the shape. Use the Word List to help you.

   _____ prism

Use Vocabulary in Writing

5. Draw some shapes. Label the shapes using words from the Word List.

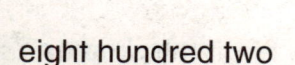

802 eight hundred two

Name _____

Set A

You can sort 2-D shapes by sides and vertices.

These have sides and vertices.

These have no sides and no vertices.

Reteaching

Solve each problem below.

1. Circle the shape that has 4 straight sides and 4 vertices.

2. Circle the shape that has 0 vertices.

Set B

You can make 2-D shapes using different kinds of materials.

Construction paper

Toothpicks

Colored sticks

Construction paper

Use materials your teacher gives you to make a rectangle. Glue or tape it in the box.

3.

Topic 14 | Reteaching

eight hundred three **803**

Set C

You can use pattern blocks to make a larger shape.

	🔺	🔷
Way 1	1	1
Way 2	3	0

4. Make this shape in two different ways.

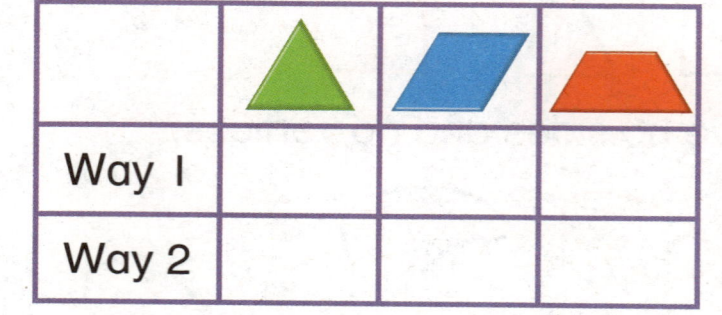

	🔺	🔷	🟧
Way 1			
Way 2			

Set D

You can use pattern blocks to make a picture.

Write the number of blocks you used.

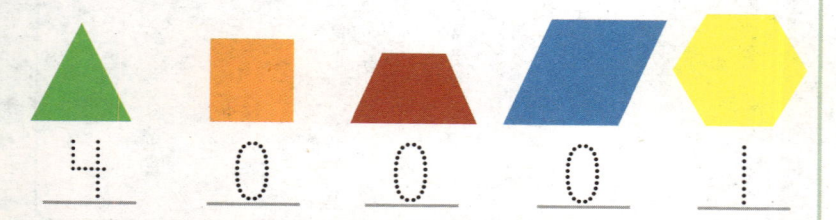

🔺	🟧	🔻	🔷	⬢
4	0	0	0	1

5. Make a picture. Write how many of each block used.

🔺	🟧	🔻	🔷	⬢
___	___	___	___	___

804 eight hundred four

Topic 14 | Reteaching

Name _____

Set E

You can find faces, flat surfaces, edges, and vertices on 3-D shapes or objects.

Reteaching Continued

6 faces
8 vertices
12 edges

0 flat surfaces
0 vertices
0 edges

Write how many flat surfaces, edges, and vertices for each shape.

6. ____ flat surfaces
____ vertices
____ edges

7.  ____ flat surface
____ vertex
____ edges

Set F

You can combine 3-D shapes to make bigger 3-D shapes.
Combine 2 cubes.

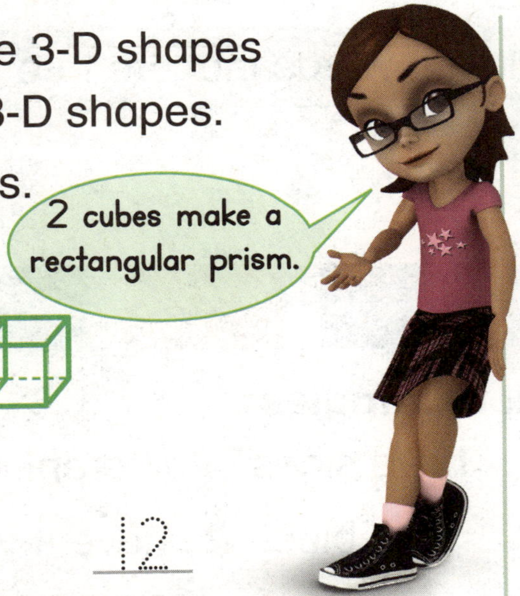

2 cubes make a rectangular prism.

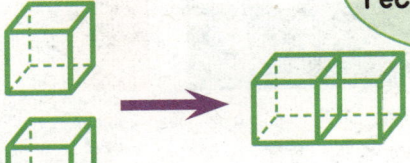

6 faces   8 vertices   12 edges

Two shapes were combined to make a new shape. Write the number of flat surfaces, vertices, and edges for the new shape.

8. 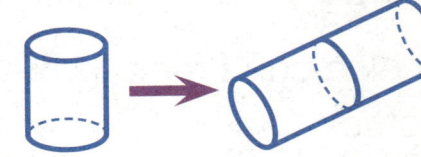 ____ flat surfaces   ____ vertices   ____ edges

Topic 14 | Reteaching

Set G

All of these are cylinders.

Cylinders are defined by:
__0__ vertices and __2__ flat surfaces.

Cylinders are **NOT** defined by:
__color__ or __direction__.

Finish the sentences to define spheres.

9. Spheres are defined by:
_____ and _____.

10. Spheres are **NOT** defined by:
_____ or _____.

Set H

Thinking Habits

Persevere

What am I asked to find?

What else can I try if I get stuck?

Circle the words that are true for all rectangles.

11. **All rectangles:**
   have sides of different lengths.
   are blue.   have 4 vertices.

Name _____

1. Which shape is a square?

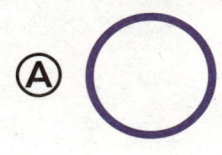

Ⓐ ○   Ⓑ △

Ⓒ ▭   Ⓓ □

2. Which shape has 3 sides?

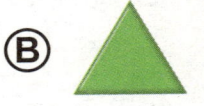

Ⓐ (trapezoid)   Ⓑ (triangle)

Ⓒ (parallelogram)   Ⓓ (square)

3. How many flat surfaces and edges does a cone have?

_____ flat surface(s)

_____ edges

4. Jaxon makes 3 triangles. Then he puts them together to make a new shape.

Draw a shape that Jaxon could have made.

Topic 14 | Assessment

eight hundred seven **807**

5. Complete the sentence. Then explain how you know you are correct.

This 3-D shape is a _____.

_____

_____

6. Jazmin is making a butterfly. Use pattern blocks to draw in the pieces she is still missing.

7. Which shows the shapes you can use to make ⬡? Choose all that apply.

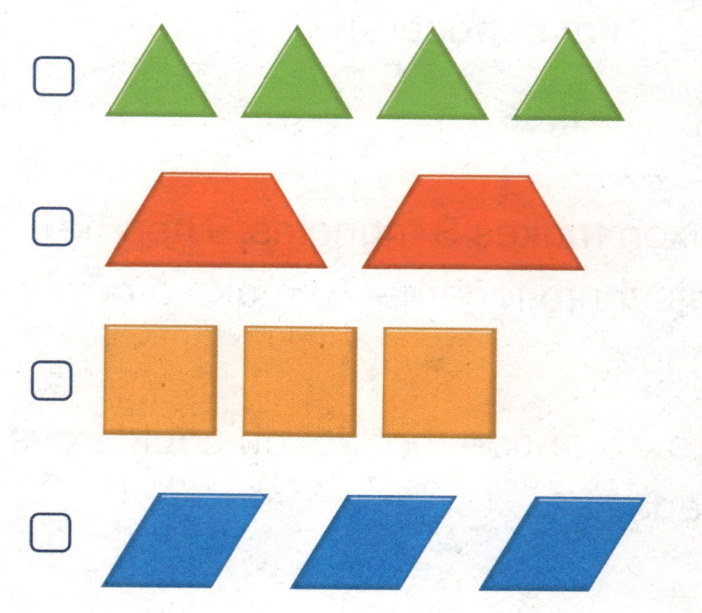

808 eight hundred eight

Name _____

8. Which 3-D shape does **NOT** have a vertex?

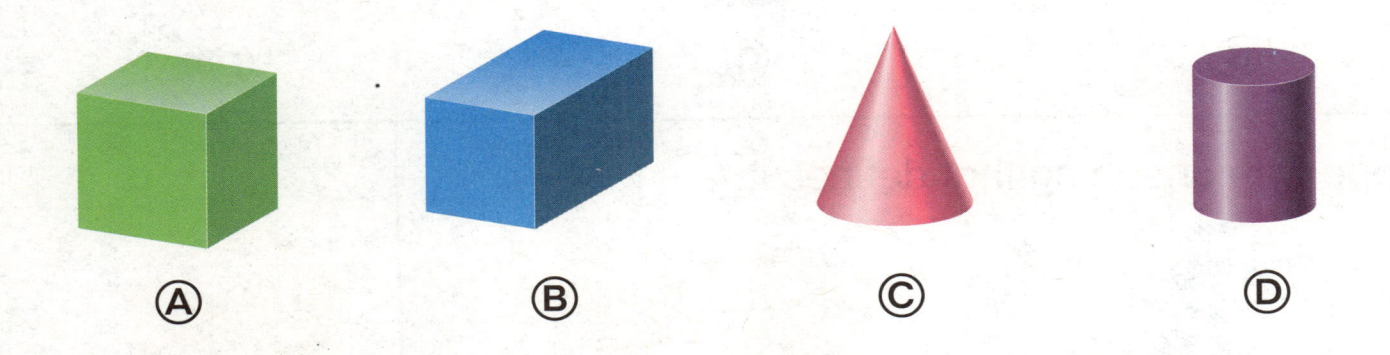

Ⓐ   Ⓑ   Ⓒ   Ⓓ

9. Which 3-D shapes can be used to make this object? Circle all that apply.

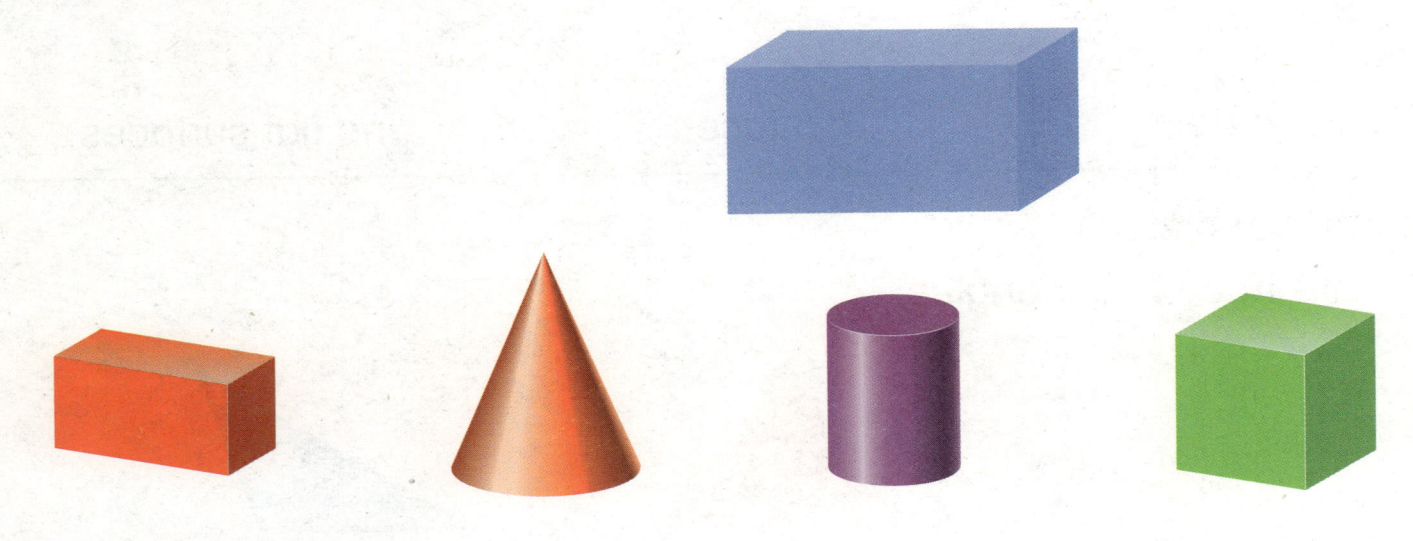

10. Which 2-D shape has no straight sides?

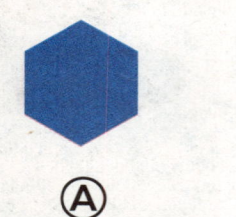

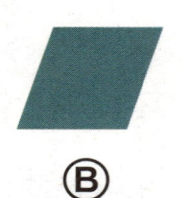

   Ⓐ   Ⓑ   Ⓒ   Ⓓ

11. Match each 3-D shape with one thing that defines it.

   12 edges   1 vertex   6 faces   no flat surfaces

12. All of these shapes are triangles.
    Circle the words that are true of all triangles.

    All triangles: have 3 sides.   are yellow.

    have 3 vertices.   are big.

810 eight hundred ten

Name _____

Home Sweet Home!

Leslie uses shapes to make this drawing of her house.

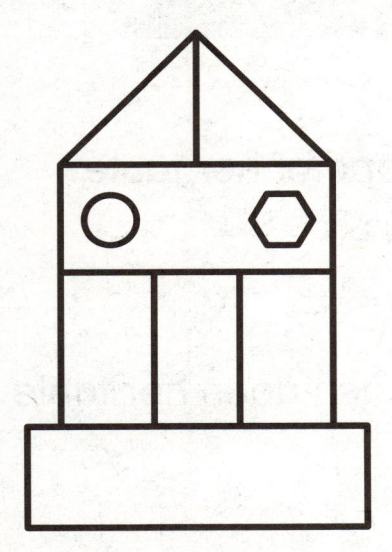

1. Color two of the rectangles in the drawing blue.

2. Explain how you know that the two shapes are rectangles.

_____

_____

3. One of the windows of the house is in the shape of a hexagon.

   Show 3 ways you could make a hexagon using smaller shapes. You can use pattern blocks to help you.

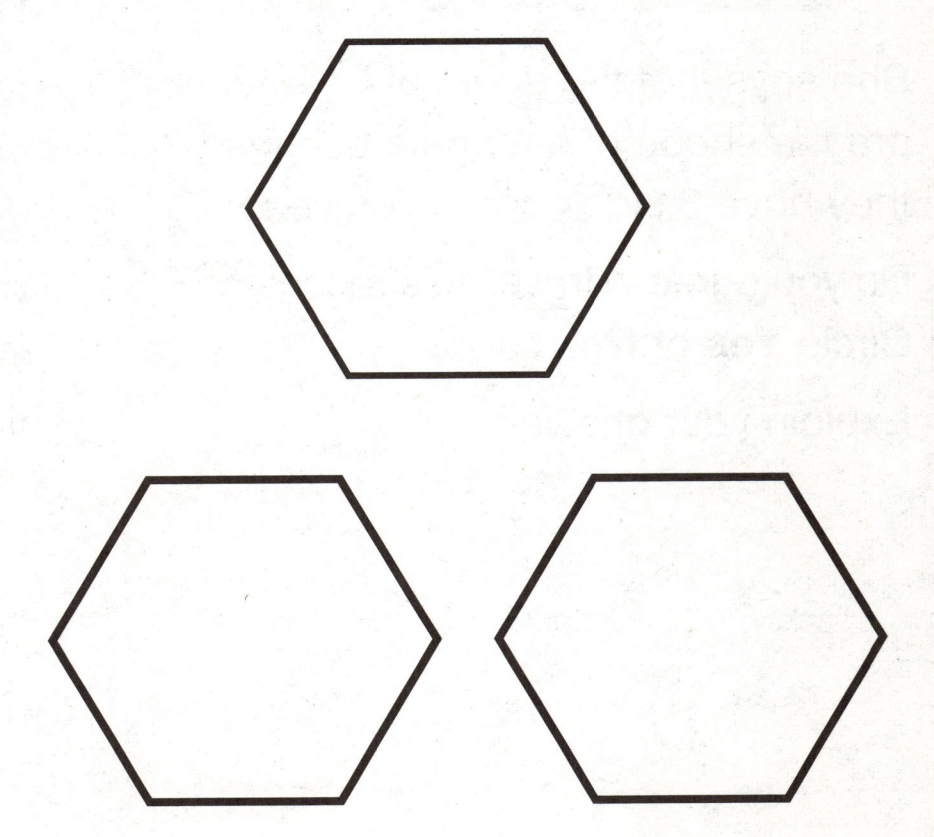

Topic 14 | Performance Assessment

eight hundred eleven 811

4. Leslie has these tents in her backyard.

She says that the doors of both tents are the shape of a triangle because they have 3 sides and 3 vertices.

Do you agree with Leslie's reasoning? Circle **Yes** or **No**.

Explain your answer.

_____
_____
_____

5. Leslie has a table in her house that is this shape.

Part A
What is the shape of her table?
_____

Part B
How many of each does her table have?

faces _____

edges _____

vertices _____

Part C
What 3-D shapes could Leslie put together to make her table?

_____
_____
_____

TOPIC 15: Equal Shares of Circles and Rectangles

Essential Question: What are some different names for equal shares?

A wheel is a perfect circle.

Wheels help us move people and things much more easily than we could otherwise.

Wow! Let's do this project and learn more.

Digital Resources: Solve, Learn, Glossary, Tools, Assessment, Help, Games

Math and Science Project: Wheels and Shapes

Find Out Talk to friends and relatives about different objects that have wheels. Ask them how they use wheels in their everyday lives.

Journal: Make a Book Show what you found out. In your book, also:
- Draw pictures of different objects that have wheels. Describe the shapes you see. How could you divide the shapes into equal shares?
- Tell how wheels are used to move people or things.

Topic 15

eight hundred thirteen **813**

Name _____

Review What You Know

Vocabulary

1. Put an X on the **circle**.

2. Draw a **rectangle**.

3. Draw the hands on the clock to show a time to the **half hour**.

Different Kinds of Rectangles

4. Color all the rectangles. Then draw an X on the rectangle that is a square.

5. How many rectangles do you see?

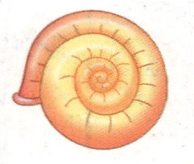

_____ rectangles

What's the Time?

6. Cody gets home at 4:00. He eats a snack a half hour later. Draw the hour and minute hands on the clock to show at what time Cody eats a snack.

814 eight hundred fourteen

Topic 15

My Word Cards

Study the words on the front of the card. Complete the activity on the back.

equal shares

There are 2 **equal shares**.

halves

The circle is divided into **halves**.

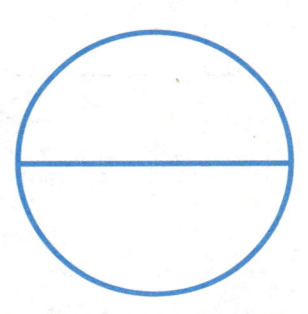

fourths

The square is divided into **fourths**.

quarters

The circle is divided into **quarters**, another word for fourths.

Topic 15 | My Word Cards

eight hundred fifteen 815

My Word Cards

Use what you know to complete the sentences. Extend learning by writing your own sentence using each word.

A whole divided into 4 equal shares is divided into _____, or quarters.

When a whole is divided into 2 equal shares, the shares are called _____.

The parts of a whole that are the same size are _____.

The 4 equal shares of a whole are called fourths or _____.

816 eight hundred sixteen

//Name _____

Lesson 15-1

Make Equal Shares

Draw a line inside the blue circle to show 2 parts that are the same size.

Draw a line inside the yellow circle to show 2 parts that are **NOT** the same size.

I can ...
determine if shapes are divided into equal shares.

I can also model with math.

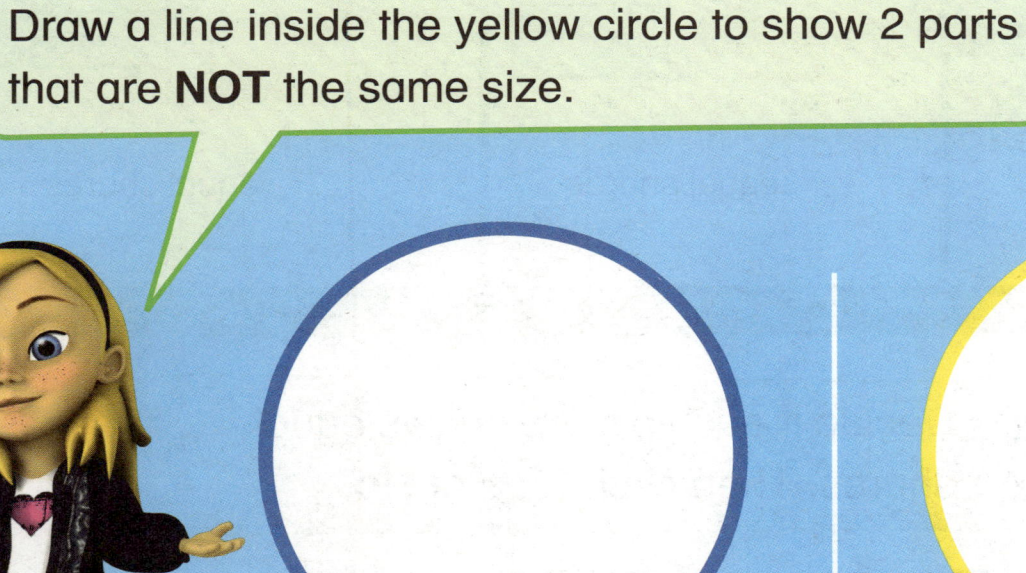

Topic 15 | Lesson 1

eight hundred seventeen 817

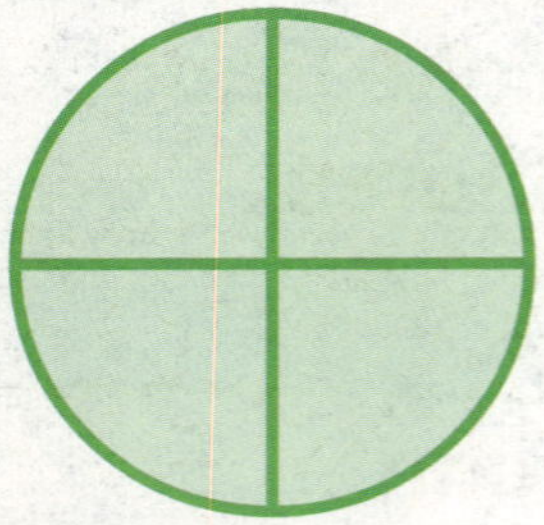

Shapes can be divided into parts, or shares. Sometimes the shares are equal.

Sometimes the shares are not equal.

Which shows 2 **equal shares**?

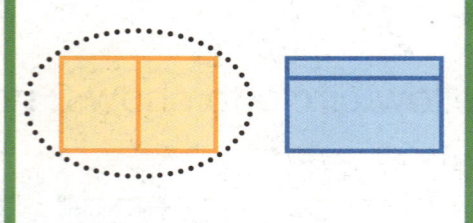

__2__ equal shares

Which shows 4 equal shares?

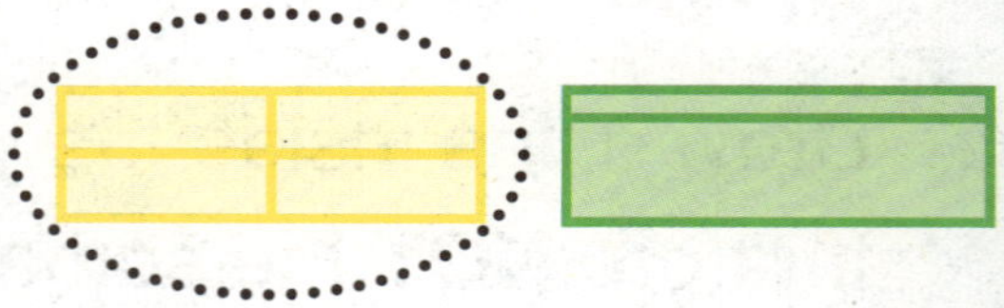

__4__ equal shares

Do You Understand?
Show Me! Is this shape divided into equal shares? Explain how you know.

Guided Practice Decide if each picture shows equal shares. Then circle **Yes** or **No**.

1. (Yes)   No

2.  Yes   No

3.  Yes   No

4.  Yes   No

5. 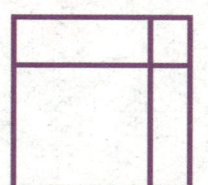 Yes   No

6. 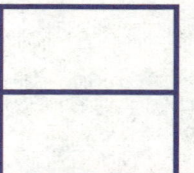 Yes   No

818 eight hundred eighteen

Topic 15 | Lesson 1

Name _____

Independent Practice

Write the number of equal shares in each shape.
If the shares are **NOT** equal, write 0.

7.  _____ equal shares

8.  _____ equal shares

9. 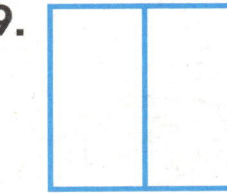 _____ equal shares

10. 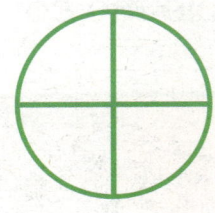 _____ equal shares

11.  _____ equal shares

12. _____ equal shares

13. 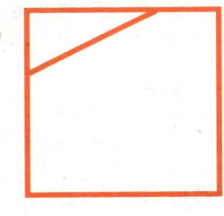 _____ equal shares

14. 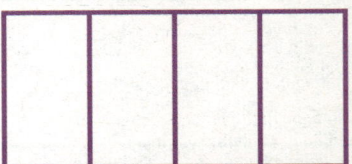 _____ equal shares

15. Higher Order Thinking Draw a square, a circle, or a rectangle. Divide your shape into equal shares. Then write the number of equal shares in your shape.

_____ equal shares

Topic 15 | Lesson 1

eight hundred nineteen 819

Problem Solving Solve each problem below.

16. Be Precise Matt makes a flag with 4 equal shares. Which flag did he make? Circle the correct flag.

17. Be Precise Ruth picks a flag with equal shares. Which flag did she pick? Circle the correct flag.

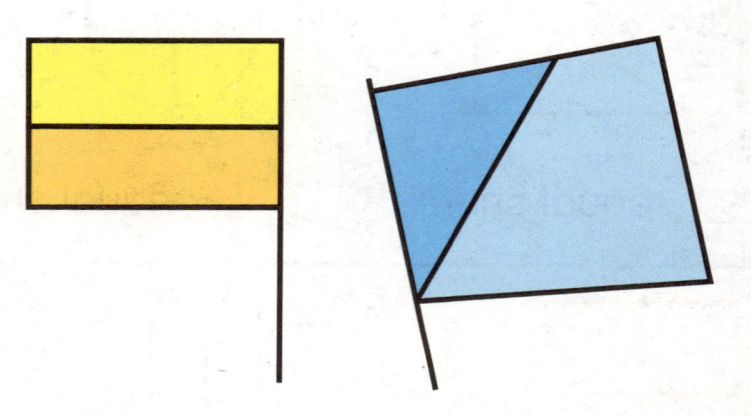

18. Higher Order Thinking 4 students share a pizza. Each pizza slice is the same size. Draw a picture of the pizza the students shared.

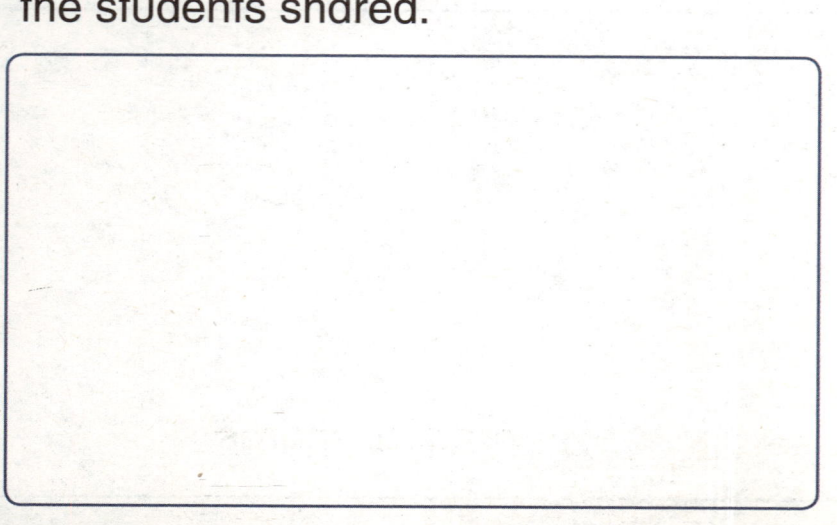

19. Assessment Which square does **NOT** show 4 equal shares?

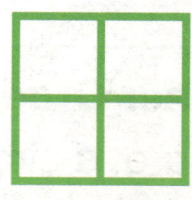

Ⓐ Ⓑ

Ⓒ Ⓓ

Name _____

Homework & Practice 15-1
Make Equal Shares

Another Look! A shape can be divided into shares that are equal or shares that are **NOT** equal.

This rectangle is divided into equal shares.

This rectangle is **NOT** divided into equal shares.

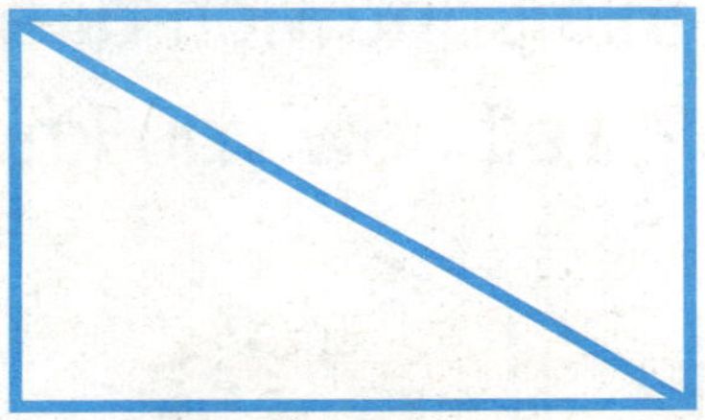

The shares are the same size.
There are 2 equal shares.

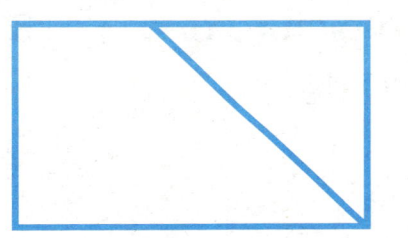

The shares are **NOT** the same size.
There are ___0___ equal shares.

HOME ACTIVITY Draw 2 squares, 2 rectangles, and 2 circles. Have your child divide 1 square, 1 rectangle, and 1 circle into equal shares and 1 square, 1 rectangle, and 1 circle into unequal shares.

Write the number of equal shares in each shape. If the shares are **NOT** equal, write 0.

1. ____ equal shares

2. ____ equal shares

3. ____ equal shares

Topic 15 | Lesson 1   Digital Resources at SavvasRealize.com   eight hundred twenty-one   821

Draw straight lines to divide the shapes into equal shares.

4.

2 equal shares

5.

4 equal shares

6.

2 equal shares

7. **Math and Science** Draw a picture of a bike wheel. Draw lines to divide it into 4 equal shares.

8. **Be Precise** Has this sandwich been cut into equal shares? Tell how you know.

9. **Higher Order Thinking** Two brothers divide a slice of bread into equal shares. One brother thinks he got a smaller share than the other. How can he check if he is right?

10. **Assessment** Which tells how many equal shares the apple has?

Ⓐ 8
Ⓑ 3
Ⓒ 4
Ⓓ 2

Name _____

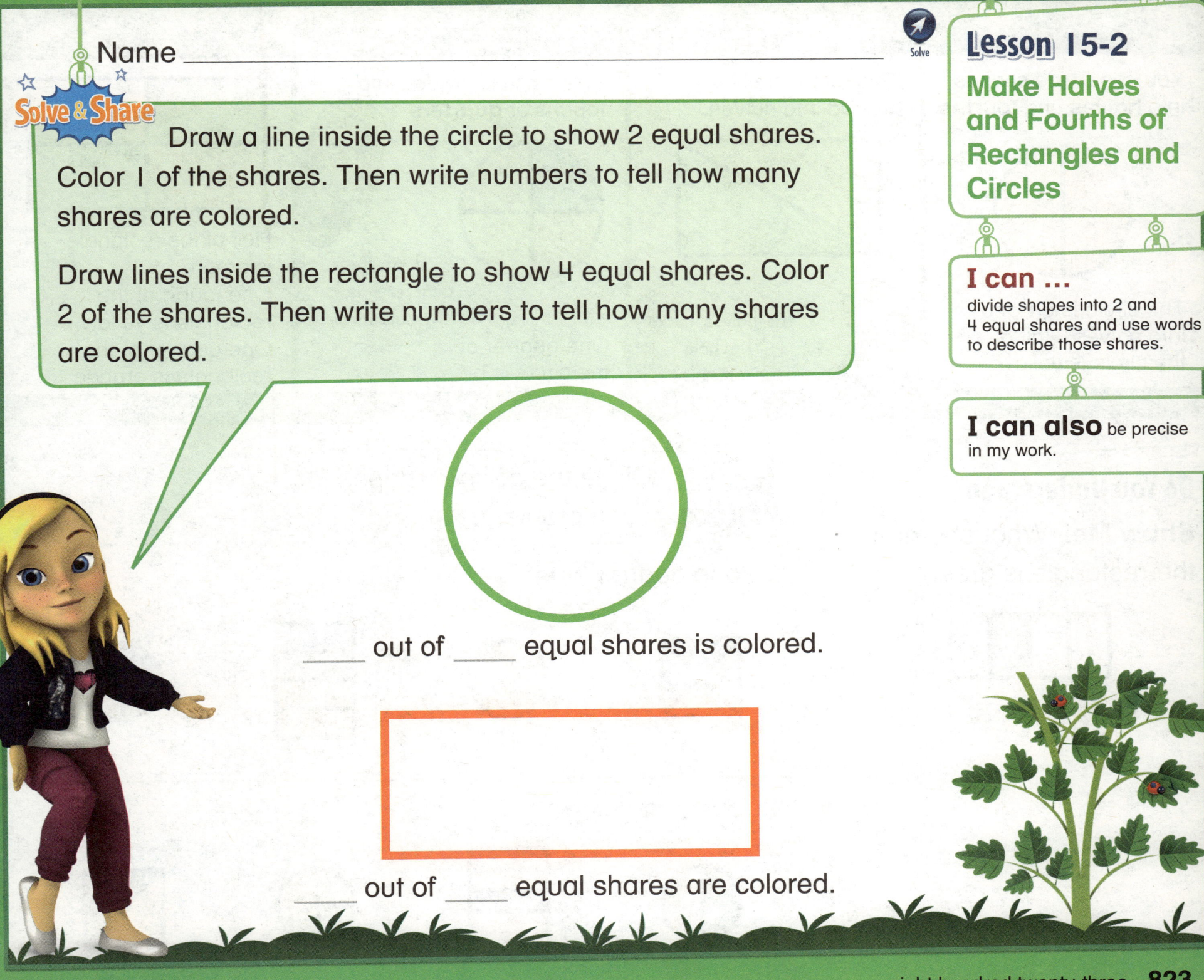

Solve & Share

Draw a line inside the circle to show 2 equal shares. Color 1 of the shares. Then write numbers to tell how many shares are colored.

Draw lines inside the rectangle to show 4 equal shares. Color 2 of the shares. Then write numbers to tell how many shares are colored.

Lesson 15-2
Make Halves and Fourths of Rectangles and Circles

I can ...
divide shapes into 2 and 4 equal shares and use words to describe those shares.

I can also be precise in my work.

____ out of ____ equal shares is colored.

____ out of ____ equal shares are colored.

Topic 15 | Lesson 2 · eight hundred twenty-three · 823

You can divide shapes into **halves** and **fourths**.

The circle is divided into halves. Half of the circle is yellow.

This rectangle is divided into halves.

"2 of the halves make 1 whole rectangle."

This circle is divided into fourths or **quarters**.

One quarter of the circle is blue.

"4 of the quarters make 1 whole circle."

Half of the rectangle is green.
One fourth of the rectangle is yellow.
One quarter of the rectangle is orange.

Do You Understand?

Show Me! What share of the rectangle is green?

Guided Practice

Circle the correct shapes for each problem.

1. one quarter blue

2. one half yellow

824 eight hundred twenty-four

Topic 15 | Lesson 2

Name _____

Independent Practice   Color the shapes for each problem.

3. one half red

4. one fourth orange

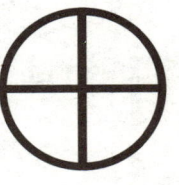

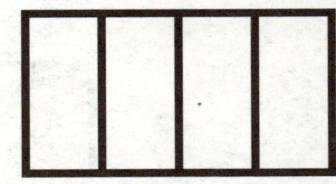

5. one quarter green

6. one half blue

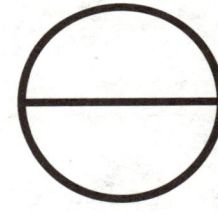

7. Number Sense Alex has one half of an oatmeal bar. Jen has one quarter of a different oatmeal bar. Jen's piece is bigger. How could Jen's piece be bigger? Use words or pictures to solve.

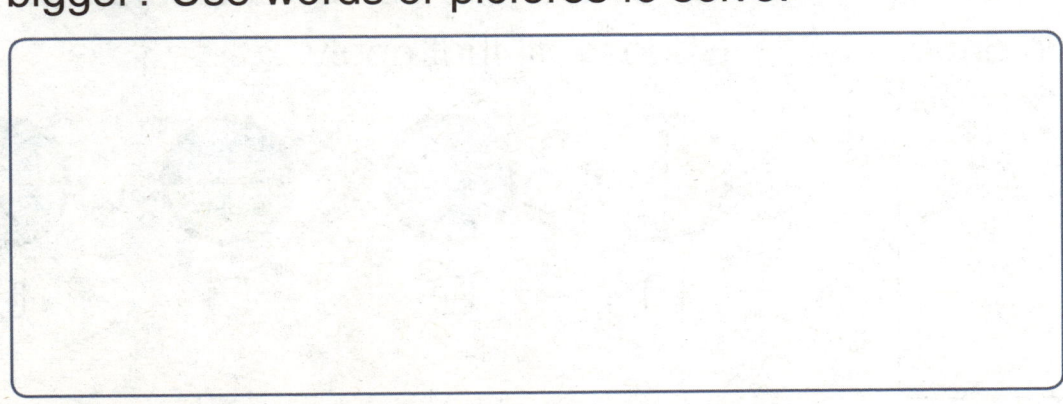

Think about the sizes of the oatmeal bars!

Topic 15 | Lesson 2

eight hundred twenty-five **825**

Problem Solving   Solve each problem below.

8. **Explain** Sam says the rectangle is divided into halves. Is he correct? Circle **Yes** or **No**. Then explain how you know.

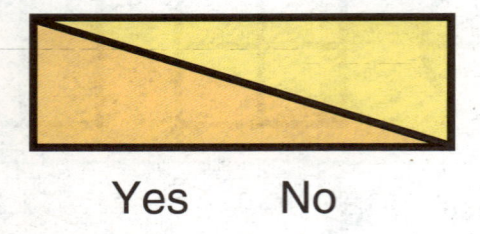

   Yes   No

9. **Explain** Mia says the circle is divided into fourths. Lucy says it is divided into quarters. Who is correct? Explain how you know.

10. **Higher Order Thinking** Dana draws a rectangle divided into fourths. She colors one half of the rectangle blue and one quarter of the rectangle green. Draw a rectangle to match the one Dana drew.

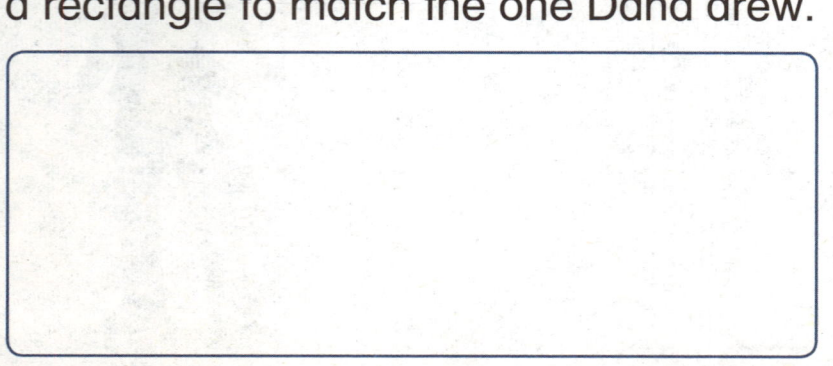

11. **Assessment** Yao colors a circle. One half of the circle is blue. The other half is **NOT** blue. Which shows the shape Yao could have colored? Choose all that apply.

Name _____

Homework & Practice 15-2
Make Halves and Fourths of Rectangles and Circles

Another Look! You can divide shapes into halves and fourths.

Two **halves** make one whole.

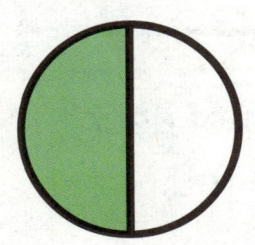

Four **fourths** make one whole.

One fourth is the same as one quarter.

Each share is called a **half**.
One **half** of the circle is green.

Each share is called a _fourth_.
One _fourth_ of the rectangle is green.
One _quarter_ of the rectangle is blue.

HOME ACTIVITY Draw a circle and a rectangle. Have your child divide the circle into two equal shares and color one share. Then have your child divide the rectangle into four equal shares and color one share. Ask: "Which shape shows one half colored? Which shape shows one fourth colored?"

Circle the correct shapes for each problem.

1. one half blue

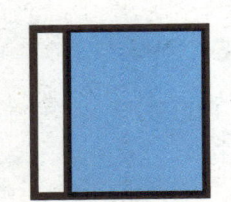

2. one quarter green

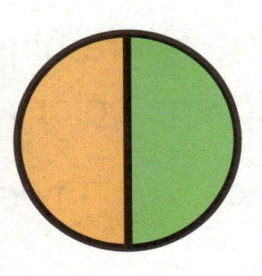

3. one half yellow

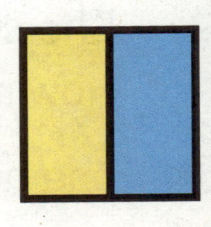

Topic 15 | Lesson 2

eight hundred twenty-seven **827**

Color the shapes for each problem.

4. one half blue

5. one quarter purple

6. one fourth red

7. Higher Order Thinking Color one half of each circle blue. Color one half of each rectangle that is **NOT** a square orange. Color one quarter of each square red.

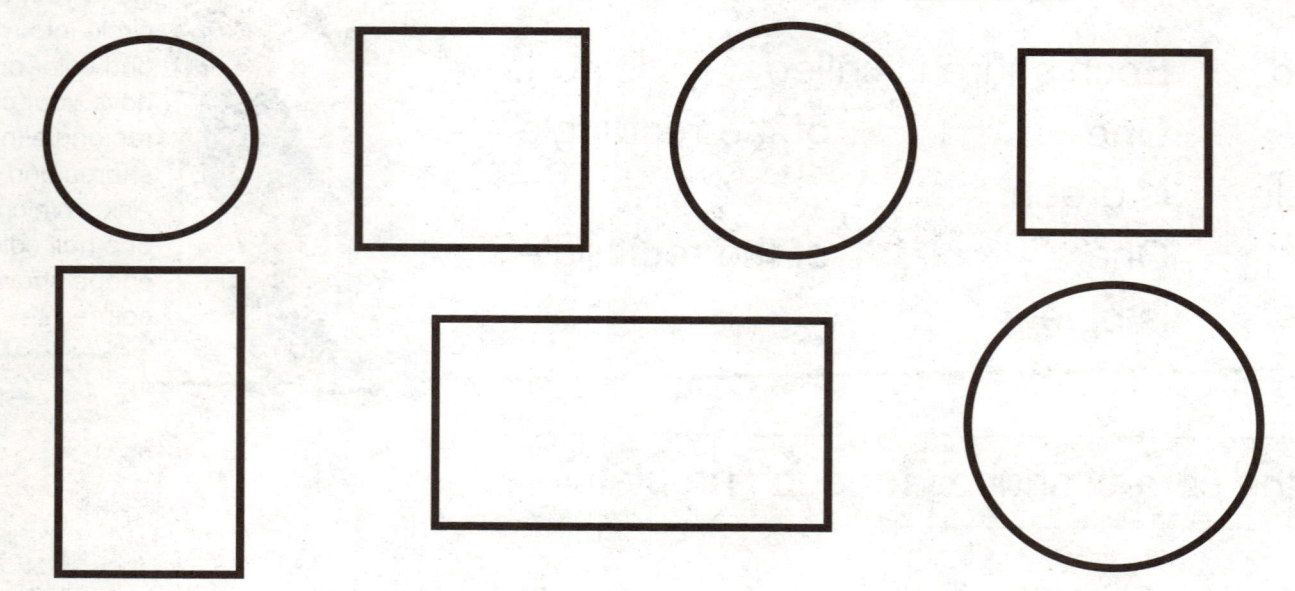

8. ✓Assessment Sandy divided a rectangle into four equal shares. She colored one share red, one share blue, and two shares yellow. How much of the rectangle did she color red? Choose all that apply.

one half ☐   one quarter ☐   two of four shares ☐   one fourth ☐

828 eight hundred twenty-eight   Topic 15 | Lesson 2

Name _____

Solve & Share

Which is larger: one half or one fourth of the same sandwich?
Divide the sandwiches. Then circle the sandwich that has larger equal shares.

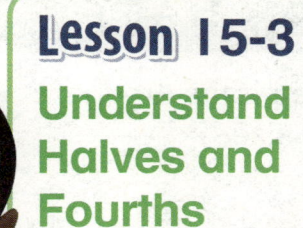

Lesson 15-3

Understand Halves and Fourths

I can ...
tell that more equal shares of the same whole creates smaller shares.

I can also reason about math.

Divide into halves

Divide into fourths

Topic 15 | Lesson 3 | Digital Resources at SavvasRealize.com | eight hundred twenty-nine **829**

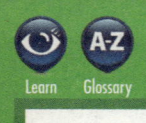

These pizzas are the same size.

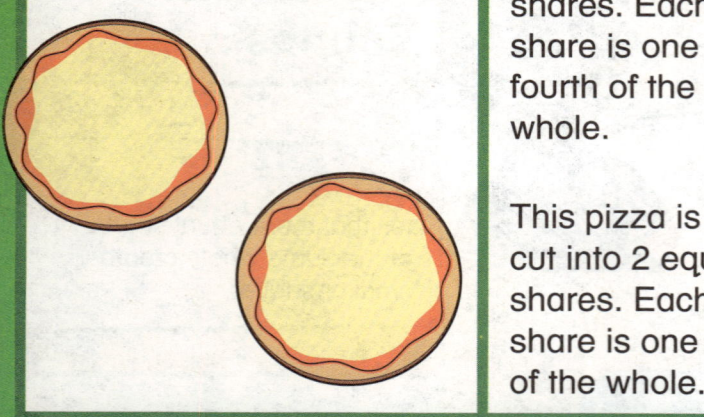

This pizza is cut into 4 equal shares. Each share is one fourth of the whole.

This pizza is cut into 2 equal shares. Each share is one half of the whole.

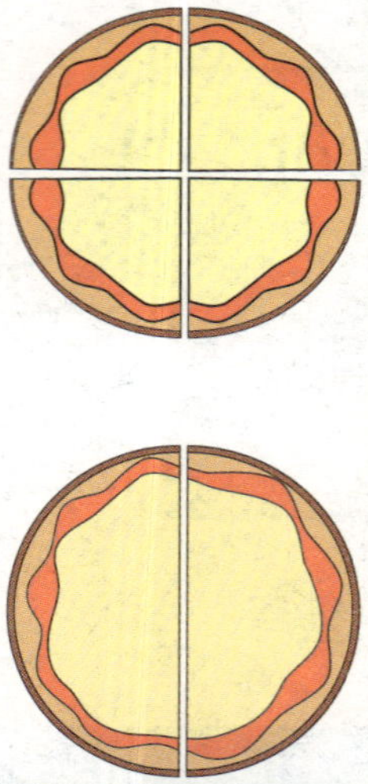

The pizza with fourths has smaller shares.

The pizza with halves has fewer shares.

Do You Understand?

Show Me! David has a sandwich. Is half of the sandwich more or less food than one fourth of the sandwich? Explain.

Guided Practice

Circle the shape that has more equal shares. Put an **X** on the shape that has larger equal shares.

1. fourths   halves

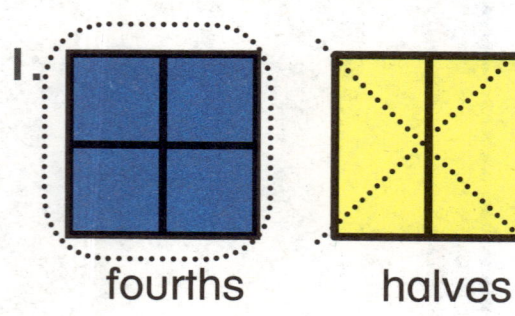

2. halves   quarters

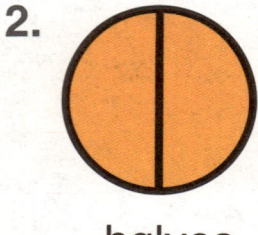

3. fourths   halves

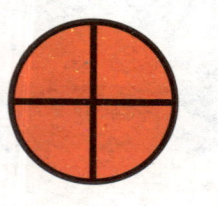

4. quarters   halves

830 eight hundred thirty

Topic 15 | Lesson 3

Name _____

Independent Practice   Solve each problem.

5. Draw a line to divide this shape in half.

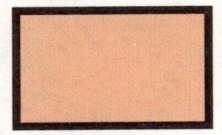

6. Shade one quarter of this shape.

7. Draw lines in the orange square to make smaller equal shares than are in the blue square.

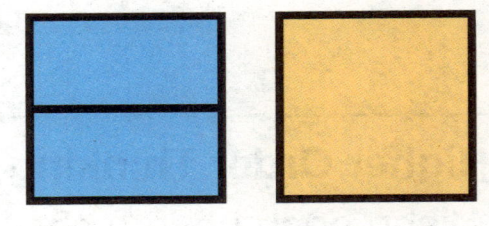

8. Higher Order Thinking Joan cuts a rectangle into 2 equal shares. Then she cuts each share in half. How many equal shares are there now? What are these shares called? Use words or pictures to explain.

Topic 15 | Lesson 3

eight hundred thirty-one 831

Problem Solving Solve each problem.

9. **Reasoning** Steve wants to cut a pan of cornbread into equal shares. Will the shares be larger if he cuts the cornbread into halves or into fourths? Use the picture to help you solve.

The larger shares will be _____.

10. **Higher Order Thinking** Burke and Alisha each have a sheet of paper. Both sheets are the same size. Burke uses one half of his sheet. Alisha uses two fourths of her sheet. Alisha says that they used equal amounts of paper.

Is she correct? Explain your answer. You can draw a picture to help.

11. **Assessment** Joey has two circles of the same size. He cuts one into halves and the other into fourths. Which words describe how the halves compare to the fourths?

smaller, more
Ⓐ

smaller, fewer
Ⓑ

larger, more
Ⓒ

larger, fewer
Ⓓ

Name _____

Homework & Practice 15-3

Understand Halves and Fourths

Another Look! These rectangles are the same size.
The rectangle with more equal shares has smaller shares.
The rectangle with fewer equal shares has larger shares.

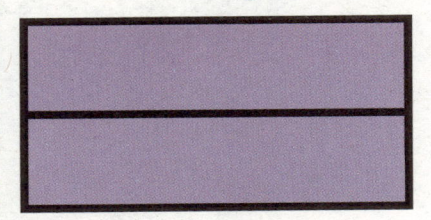

__2__ equal shares
halves
larger equal shares

__4__ equal shares
fourths
smaller equal shares

HOME ACTIVITY Draw two circles that are the same size. Ask your child to draw lines to divide one circle into halves and one circle into fourths. Then ask your child which circle has more equal shares and which circle has larger equal shares.

Compare the two shapes. Draw lines where you need to. Tell how many equal shares. Then circle **smaller** or **larger** and **more** or **fewer** for each.

1. quarters

equal shares:
smaller   larger
more   fewer

____ equal shares

halves

equal shares:
smaller   larger
more   fewer

____ equal shares

Topic 15 | Lesson 3

eight hundred thirty-three 833

2. **Reasoning** Ginny and Martha each have a pizza. Their pizzas are the same size.
Ginny cuts her pizza into fourths. Martha cuts her pizza into halves.

Who has more slices? _____

Who has larger slices? _____

3. **Vocabulary** Divide this square into **halves**. Then shade one half of the square.

4. **Higher Order Thinking** Lucas divides a circle into 2 equal shares. Then he divides each share in half. How many equal shares are there now? What are they called? Use words and pictures to explain.

5. **Assessment** Mary is designing a sign. She wants one half of the sign to be red, one fourth of it to be blue, and one quarter of it to be yellow.

Which shows what Mary's sign might look like?

Ⓐ Ⓑ

Ⓒ Ⓓ

Name _____

Solve & Share

Mary's blanket is divided into 2 equal shares. One share of the blanket is yellow and the other is orange. How can you describe the share of the blanket that is yellow? Complete the sentences below. Then draw and color the blanket to show your work.

Problem Solving
Lesson 15-4
Model with Math

I can ...
make a drawing or diagram to show a problem about equal shares.

I can also use numbers to describe equal shares.

Thinking Habits
Can I use a drawing, diagram, table, graph, or objects to show the problem?

One _____ of the blanket is yellow.
____ of the ____ shares is yellow.

Topic 15 | Lesson 4   eight hundred thirty-five **835**

Miss Rose's curtain is divided into 4 equal shares. She dyes 2 shares red and 2 shares blue.

How can you describe the shares of the curtain that are red?

Can pictures and objects be used to show the problem?

I can draw a picture of the curtain with 4 equal shares.

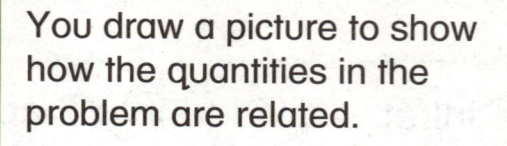

You draw a picture to show how the quantities in the problem are related.

I can color in the equal shares to match the problem.

You can use words to describe the drawing.

The drawing shows 4 equal shares. 2 of 4 shares are red.

Do You Understand?

Show Me! Amy buys a green and blue rug. It is divided into 4 equal shares. Half of the rug is green. The rest is blue. How many shares are blue? How do you know?

Guided Practice

Draw a picture to solve the problem. Then complete the sentence.

1. Pete makes a purple and yellow flag. The flag is divided into fourths. 2 shares are yellow. The rest of the flag is purple. How many of the shares are purple?

   _2_ out of _4_ equal shares are purple.

836 eight hundred thirty-six

Topic 15 | Lesson 4

Name _____

Independent Practice   Draw a picture to solve each problem. Then complete the sentence.

2. Tracy's pizza is cut into halves. She eats 1 of the shares. How many shares of the pizza does she eat?

   Tracy eats _____ out of _____ equal shares.

3. Mia cut her sandwich into quarters. 2 of the shares have cheese. What share of the sandwich does **NOT** have cheese?

   _____ out of _____ shares do not have cheese.

4. **Algebra** Color the correct number of shares to continue the pattern.

Topic 15 | Lesson 4

eight hundred thirty-seven   837

Problem Solving

✓ **Performance Assessment**

Pizza Shares Kim cuts a pizza into 4 equal shares. She gives half of the pizza to Stephen.

5. **Model** Draw a picture to show the shares of the pizza that Stephen has.

6. **Reasoning** How many shares of the pizza are left after Kim gives half to Stephen? Write the missing numbers.

   _____ out of _____ shares are left.

7. **Explain** What if Kim gives Stephen only 1 share of the pizza? Explain how you can find the number of shares that Kim has left.

_____

_____

_____

838 eight hundred thirty-eight

Topic 15 | Lesson 4

Name _____

Homework & Practice 15-4
Model with Math

Another Look! Dale's flag is divided into 4 equal shares. 2 of the shares are yellow. The rest are green. How many shares of Dale's flag are green?

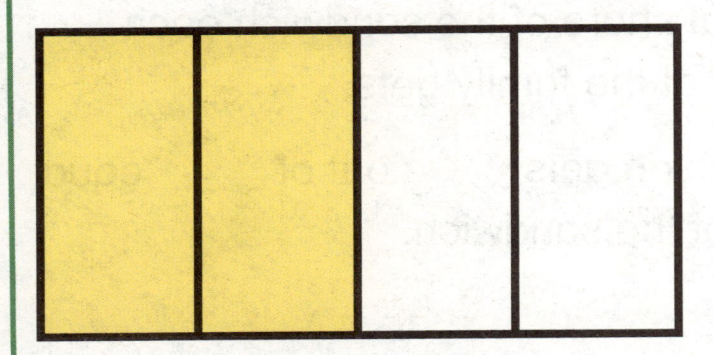

The picture can help you see that the shares that are not shaded must be green.

So, __2__ out of 4 shares will be green.

A picture can help you solve the problem. You can use the math words you know to write a sentence to solve the problem.

HOME ACTIVITY Read this story to your child: "Jack has a mat with four equal shares. Two shares are green. How many shares are not green?" Have your child draw a picture to solve the problem. Ask him or her to solve similar stories. Then write a sentence that goes with each number story.

Draw a picture to solve the problem. Then complete the sentences.

1. Sasha's scarf is divided into halves. One of the shares is brown. The rest of the scarf is green.

   ____ out of ____ equal shares is brown.

   ____ out of ____ equal shares is green.

Topic 15 | Lesson 4

Performance Assessment

Sandwich Shares The Dawson family buys 1 big sandwich to share equally. There are 4 members of the family.

2. **Model** Draw a picture to show how the family members can share the sandwich.

3. **Reasoning** Complete the sentence that tells what share of the sandwich each member of the family gets.

   Each person gets _____ out of _____ equal shares of the sandwich.

4. **Explain** Rachel is a member of the Dawson family. She gives her share of the sandwich to her brother Gary. What share of the sandwich does Gary have now? Explain how you found the answer using words or pictures.

Name _____

Find a Match

Find a partner. Point to a clue. Read the clue. Look below the clues to find a match. Write the clue letter in the box next to the match. Find a match for every clue.

TOPIC 15 Fluency Practice Activity

I can ... add and subtract within 10.

Clues

A 4 + 2 + 1

B 4 − 1

C 5 − 3

D 2 + 2 + 2

E 5 − 1

F 1 + 3 + 1

G 4 + 4

H 1 + 3 + 6

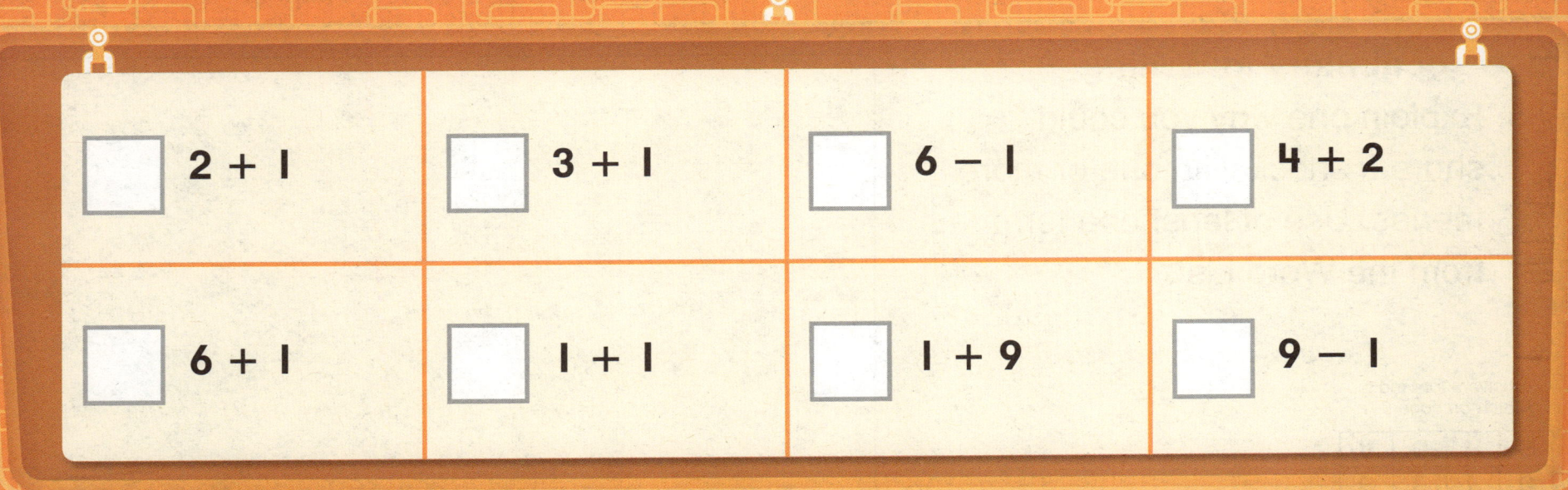

| ☐ 2 + 1 | ☐ 3 + 1 | ☐ 6 − 1 | ☐ 4 + 2 |
| ☐ 6 + 1 | ☐ 1 + 1 | ☐ 1 + 9 | ☐ 9 − 1 |

Topic 15 | Fluency Practice Activity

Answers for Find a Match on next page.
eight hundred forty-one 841

TOPIC 15 Vocabulary Review

Word List
- equal shares
- fourths
- halves
- quarters

Understand Vocabulary

1. Fill in the blank.

   I can cut my sandwich into two equal parts called _____.

2. Fill in the blank.

   When you share a sandwich equally with three other people, you cut it into _____.

3. Fill in the blank.

   If you want everyone to get the same amount of a sandwich, you need to cut it into _____.

4. Fill in the blank.

   Four people share one whole carton of juice and each person gets the same amount. The whole carton is divided into _____.

Use Vocabulary in Writing

5. Explain one way you could share a snack with one or more friends. Use at least one term from the Word List.

Answers for Find a Match on page 841

A	C	H	G
B	E	F	D

Name _____

Set A

You can divide a whole into shares.

4 equal shares

0 equal shares

Write the number of equal shares in each shape. If the shares are **NOT** equal, write 0.

1. 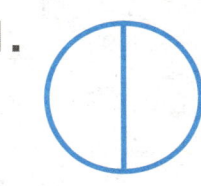 ____ equal shares

2.  ____ equal shares

Set B

You can divide shapes into equal shares. You can describe the shares using the words *half* or *fourth*.

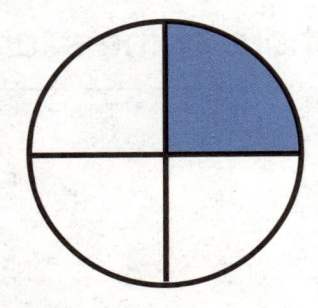

one *fourth* blue

Divide and color the shapes for each problem.

3. one half green

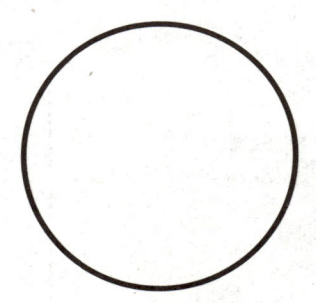

4. one fourth orange

TOPIC 15 | Reteaching

Set C

You can compare shares of the same shape that are different sizes.

These circles are the same size, but they are divided differently.

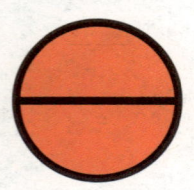

The red circle has larger equal shares.
The yellow circle has more equal shares.

Divide the shapes. Then circle the words that complete the sentences.

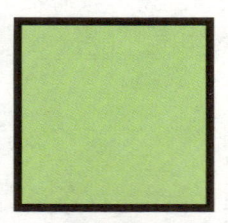

quarters   halves

5. The blue square has **smaller / larger** equal shares than the green square.

6. The green square has **more / fewer** equal shares than the blue square.

Set D

Thinking Habits

Model with Math

How can I use math words I know to help solve the problem?

Can I use a drawing, diagram, table, graph, or objects to show the problem?

Draw a picture to solve the problem.

7. Maya's scarf is divided into 4 equal shares. 1 share is green. 2 shares are yellow. The rest is blue. What share of the scarf is blue?

_____ out of _____ equal shares is blue.

Name _____

1. Which shape shows 2 equal shares?

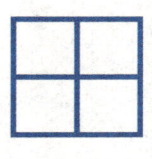

   Ⓐ   Ⓑ   Ⓒ   Ⓓ

2. Which shape does **NOT** show one fourth colored blue?

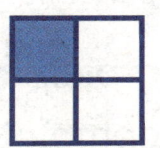

   Ⓐ   Ⓑ   Ⓒ   Ⓓ

3. Divide the rectangle into halves. Then color half of the rectangle. Explain how you know that you colored the right amount.

Topic 15 | Assessment

eight hundred forty-five **845**

4. Which shape is divided into quarters?

Ⓐ Ⓑ Ⓒ Ⓓ

5. Compare the two shapes. Circle the words that describe the equal shares.

quarters   larger equal shares

halves   smaller equal shares

quarters   larger equal shares

halves   smaller equal shares

6. Ron draws a flag divided into 4 equal shares. 2 shares are purple and the rest are blue. How many shares of the flag are blue?

Draw a picture to solve the problem. Then complete the sentence.

_____ out of _____ equal shares are blue.

Name _____

Kerry's Kitchen

Kerry loves to cook!
She makes many different foods.

1. Kerry bakes a loaf of bread.
   She cuts it into equal shares.
   How many equal shares are there?

   _____ equal shares

2. Kerry makes a pizza.
   She cuts it so that she and her sister each get an equal share.
   What are the shares called?

   _____

   Show two ways that Kerry could divide the pizza.

3. Kerry makes a sandwich.
   She eats one half of it.
   Color to show how much she ate.

   How many halves make the whole sandwich?

   _____ halves

   Think about what "half" means.

Topic 15 | Performance Assessment

eight hundred forty-seven 847

4. Kerry makes a pan of oatmeal bars.
   She cuts up the bars.
   Kerry says that she divided the bars into fourths.

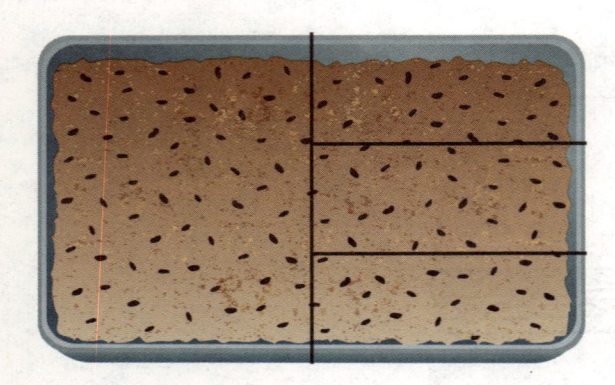

   Is she correct?   Circle **Yes** or **No**.

   Explain your answer.

   _____
   _____
   _____

5. Kerry makes a salad.
   She cuts a tomato into four equal shares.
   She puts 1 equal share of the tomato in the salad.

   Part A
   Draw a picture to show the share of the tomato that is in the salad.

   Part B
   The equal shares that Kerry cut are called fourths.
   What is another name for these shares?

   _____

   Part C
   How many fourths are in the whole tomato?

   There are _____ fourths in the whole tomato.

848 eight hundred forty-eight

STEP UP to Grade 2

Here's a preview of next year. These lessons help you step up to Grade 2.

Lessons

1 Even and Odd Numbers **851**

2 Use Arrays to Find Totals **855**

3 Add on a Hundred Chart **859**

4 Models to Add 2-Digit Numbers **863**

5 Subtract on a Hundred Chart **867**

6 Models to Subtract 2- and 1-Digit Numbers **871**

7 Tell Time to Five Minutes **875**

8 Understand Hundreds **879**

9 Counting Hundreds, Tens, and Ones **883**

10 Skip Count by 5, 10, and 100, to 1,000 .... **887**

Name _____

Solve & Share

Use cubes to make the numbers below. Shade all the numbers that can be shown as two equal groups of cubes.
What do you notice about the numbers you shaded?

Step Up to Grade 2

Lesson 1
Even and Odd Numbers

I can ...
tell if a group of objects is even or odd.

I can also use math tools correctly.

1	2	3	4	5	6	7	8	9	10
11	12	13	14	15	16	17	18	19	20

Step Up | Lesson 1

How can you tell if a number is **even** or **odd**?

"Use cubes to find out."

8
9

An even number can be shown as two equal parts using cubes.

8 is even.
4 + 4 = 8

An odd number cannot be shown as two equal parts using cubes.

9 is odd.
5 + 4 = 9

The ones digit tells you if a number is even or odd.

"18 is even.
19 is odd."

| 1 | 2 | 3 | 4 | 5 | 6 | 7 | 8 | 9 | 10 |
| 11 | 12 | 13 | 14 | 15 | 16 | 17 | 18 | 19 | 20 |

Do You Understand?

Show Me! You break apart a tower of cubes to make two equal parts, but there is one cube left over. Is the number of cubes even or odd? Explain.

Guided Practice

Look at the number. Circle even or odd. Then write the equation.

1. 8

   odd   (even)

   4 + 4 = 8

2. 11

   odd   even

   ___ + ___ = ___

852 eight hundred fifty-two

Step Up | Lesson 1

Name _____

Independent Practice

Look at the number. Circle even or odd.
Then write the equation. Use cubes to help.

3. 9

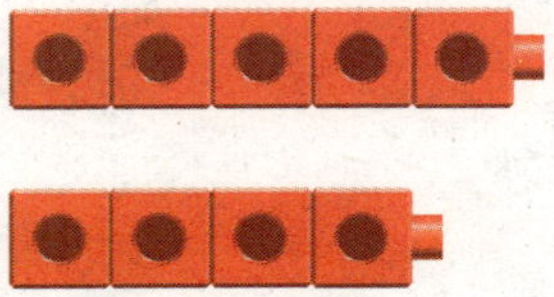

odd   even

___ + ___ = ___

4. 18

odd   even

___ + ___ = ___

5. 10

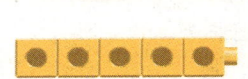

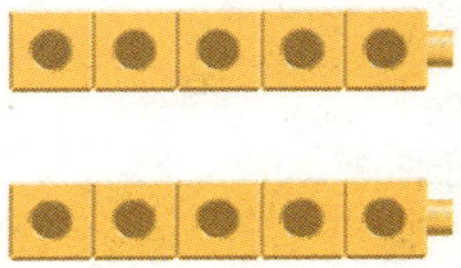

odd   even

___ + ___ = ___

6. 13

odd   even

___ + ___ = ___

7. 7

odd   even

___ + ___ = ___

8. 6

odd   even

___ + ___ = ___

For each number, circle true or false. Then explain your thinking.

9. **Higher Order Thinking**
Carl says 14 is even.
He says 41 is odd.
True or false?

14
True
False

41
True
False

_____
_____
_____
_____

Step Up | Lesson 1

eight hundred fifty-three 853

Problem Solving
Solve the problems below. Use cubes to help.

10. Model with Math Lily fills 2 baskets with 7 berries each. She gives both baskets to Ted. Does Ted have an odd or even number of berries? Draw a picture to solve. Then write an equation.

____ + ____ = ____

Ted has an _____ number of berries.

11. Model with Math Peter puts 8 marbles in one jar. He puts 1 marble in another jar. Does Peter have an odd or even number of marbles? Draw a picture to solve. Then write an equation.

____ + ____ = ____

Peter has an _____ number of marbles.

12. Higher Order Thinking If you add two even numbers, will the sum be odd or even? Explain. Use numbers, pictures, or words.

13. Assessment Use the numbers on the cards below. Write two different addition equations. The sum in each equation needs to be an odd number.

| 1 | 7 | 2 | 8 |

____ + ____ = ____   ____ + ____ = ____

854   eight hundred fifty-four

Step Up | Lesson 1

Name _____

Solve & Share

Show and explain two different ways to find how many circles in all.

Step Up to Grade 2

Lesson 2
Use Arrays to Find Totals

I can ...
find the total number of objects in a set of rows and columns.

I can also look for patterns.

Step Up | Lesson 2   Digital Resources at SavvasRealize.com   eight hundred fifty-five **855**

You can model repeated addition with an **array**.

Arrays have equal **rows**. Each row has 3 strawberries.

Arrays have equal **columns**. Each column has 2 strawberries.

Write two equations that match the array.

By Rows
$3 + 3 = 6$

By Columns
$2 + 2 + 2 = 6$

Do You Understand?

Show Me! Is this group an array? Explain.

Guided Practice

Write two equations that match each array.

1.

By Rows

$2 + 2 = 4$

By Columns

$2 + 2 = 4$

2.

By Rows

___ + ___ + ___ = ___

By Columns

___ + ___ = ___

856 eight hundred fifty-six

Name _____

Independent Practice — Write two equations that match each array.

3.

By Rows ____ + ____ + ____ + ____ = ____

By Columns ____ + ____ + ____ = ____

4.

____ + ____ = ____

____ + ____ + ____ + ____ = ____

5.

By Rows ____ + ____ = ____

By Columns ____ + ____ + ____ = ____

6.

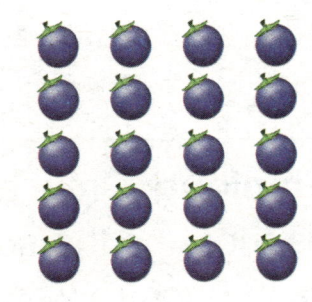

____ + ____ + ____ + ____ + ____ = ____

____ + ____ + ____ + ____ = ____

7. **Algebra** Use the array to find the missing number.

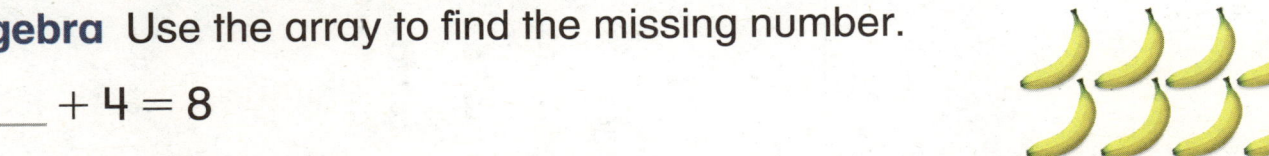

____ + 4 = 8

Step Up | Lesson 2

eight hundred fifty-seven 857

Problem Solving Use an array to solve each problem.

8. **Look for Patterns** Dana places the berries in an array. Write two equations that match the array. How many berries are there in all?

   _____

   _____

   _____ berries

9. The array shows cars in a parking lot. Can you write two different equations that match the array? Explain. How many cars are in the parking lot in all?

   _____

   _____

   _____ cars

10. **Higher Order Thinking** Draw a garden with up to 6 rows that has the same number of plants in each row. Then write two equations that match your array.

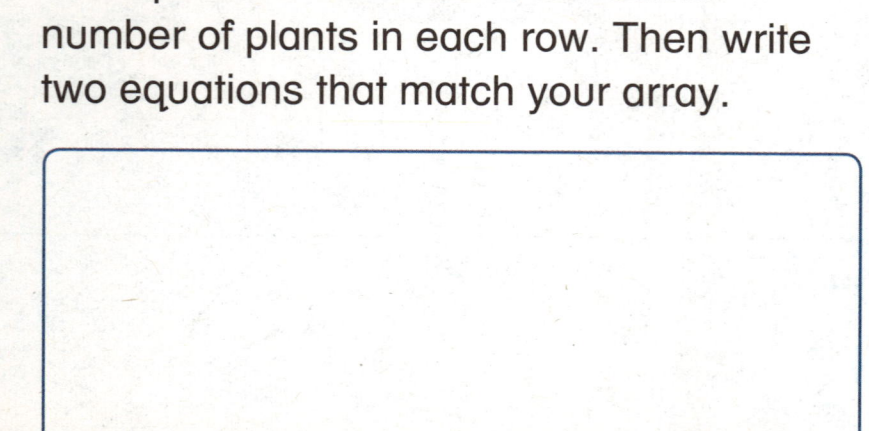

11. **Assessment** Brent sets basketballs in an array. He has 3 rows of basketballs with 4 basketballs in each row. Which equation shows the array Brent made and how many basketballs in all?

    Ⓐ $3 + 3 + 3 = 9$

    Ⓑ $3 + 3 = 6$

    Ⓒ $4 + 4 = 8$

    Ⓓ $4 + 4 + 4 = 12$

858 eight hundred fifty-eight

Step Up | Lesson 2

Name _____

Solve & Share

How can you use the hundred chart to help you solve 32 + 43? Explain. Write an addition equation to show the sum.

Step Up to Grade 2

Lesson 3
Add on a Hundred Chart

I can ...
add two-digit numbers to two-digit numbers using a hundred chart.

I can also model with math.

1	2	3	4	5	6	7	8	9	10
11	12	13	14	15	16	17	18	19	20
21	22	23	24	25	26	27	28	29	30
31	32	33	34	35	36	37	38	39	40
41	42	43	44	45	46	47	48	49	50
51	52	53	54	55	56	57	58	59	60
61	62	63	64	65	66	67	68	69	70
71	72	73	74	75	76	77	78	79	80
81	82	83	84	85	86	87	88	89	90
91	92	93	94	95	96	97	98	99	100

____ + ____ = ____

Step Up | Lesson 3

You can add on a hundred chart. Find 54 + 18.

Start at 54. You need to add the tens from 18. Move down 1 row to show 1 ten.

51	52	53	54	55	56	57	58	59	60
61	62	63	64	65	66	67	68	69	70
71	72	73	74	75	76	77	78	79	80

Now add the ones.

You're already at 64. Now move ahead 8 to show 8 ones. You need to go to the next row to add them all. So, 54 + 18 = 72.

51	52	53	54	55	56	57	58	59	60
61	62	63	64	65	66	67	68	69	70
71	72	73	74	75	76	77	78	79	80

Do You Understand?

Show Me! How can you use a hundred chart to add 35 and 24?

☆ Guided Practice ☆

Add using the hundred chart. Draw arrows on the chart if needed.

11	12	13	14	15	16	17	18	19	20
21	22	23	24	25	26	27	28	29	30
31	32	33	34	35	36	37	38	39	40
41	42	43	44	45	46	47	48	49	50

1. 14 + 32 = 46

2. 22 + 14 = ___

3. ___ = 11 + 20

4. 16 + 33 = ___

860 eight hundred sixty

Name _____

Independent Practice — Add using the hundred chart.

1	2	3	4	5	6	7	8	9	10
11	12	13	14	15	16	17	18	19	20
21	22	23	24	25	26	27	28	29	30
31	32	33	34	35	36	37	38	39	40
41	42	43	44	45	46	47	48	49	50
51	52	53	54	55	56	57	58	59	60
61	62	63	64	65	66	67	68	69	70
71	72	73	74	75	76	77	78	79	80
81	82	83	84	85	86	87	88	89	90
91	92	93	94	95	96	97	98	99	100

5. $23 + 44 =$ _____

6. _____ $= 17 + 51$

7. $28 + 21 =$ _____

8. $16 + 62 =$ _____

9. $33 + 38 =$ _____

10. $29 + 37 =$ _____

11. _____ $= 31 + 17$

12. **Higher Order Thinking** Write the digit that makes each equation true.

$52 + 2\square = 75$

$1\square + 81 = 97$

$38 + \square 1 = 59$

Step Up | Lesson 3

eight hundred sixty-one 861

Problem Solving Use the hundred chart to solve each problem.

13. **Look for Patterns** Jada has 37 buttons. Mary has 58 buttons. How many buttons do they have in all?

   _____ buttons

14. **Look for Patterns** Matt has 40 buttons. Nick has 21 more buttons than Matt. How many buttons does Nick have?

   _____ buttons

31	32	33	34	35	36	37	38	39	40
41	42	43	44	45	46	47	48	49	50
51	52	53	54	55	56	57	58	59	60
61	62	63	64	65	66	67	68	69	70
71	72	73	74	75	76	77	78	79	80
81	82	83	84	85	86	87	88	89	90
91	92	93	94	95	96	97	98	99	100

15. **Higher Order Thinking** 53 plus what number equals 84? Write the steps you take on a hundred chart to find out.

16. **Assessment** Which weights will balance the weights already on the scale?

   Ⓐ 17, 25
   Ⓑ 20, 27
   Ⓒ 11, 36
   Ⓓ 38, 12

Name _____

Solve & Share

Leslie collects 36 rocks. Her brother collects 27 rocks. How many rocks do they collect in all? Use cubes to help you solve. Draw your cubes. Tell if you need to regroup.

Step Up to Grade 2

Lesson 4
Models to Add 2-Digit Numbers

I can ...
use models to add 2 two-digit numbers and then explain my work.

I can also use math tools correctly.

Tens	Ones
+	

Regroup?
Yes   No

Step Up | Lesson 4 — eight hundred sixty-three — 863

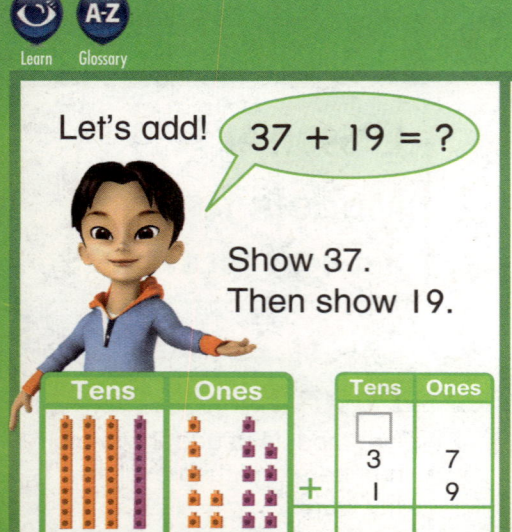

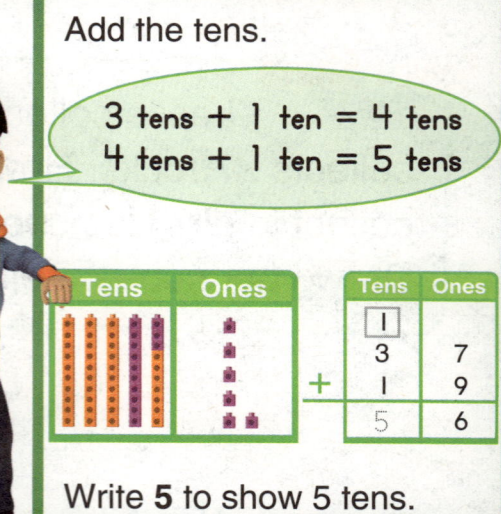

Let's add! 37 + 19 = ?

Show 37. Then show 19.

Add the ones.

7 ones + 9 ones = 16 ones

There are 16 ones. Regroup 16 ones as 1 ten and 6 ones.

Write 6 ones. Write 1 to show 1 ten.

Add the tens.

3 tens + 1 ten = 4 tens
4 tens + 1 ten = 5 tens

Write 5 to show 5 tens.

Do You Understand?

Show Me! When do you have to regroup when adding?

Guided Practice

Add. Use connecting cubes and your workmat. Did you need to regroup? Circle **Yes** or **No**.

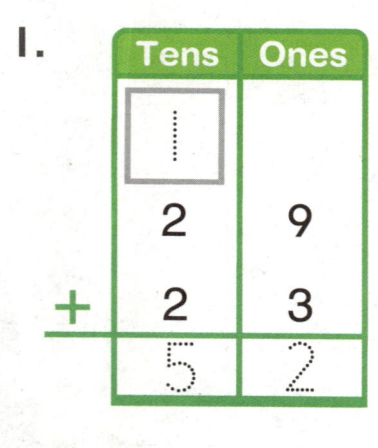

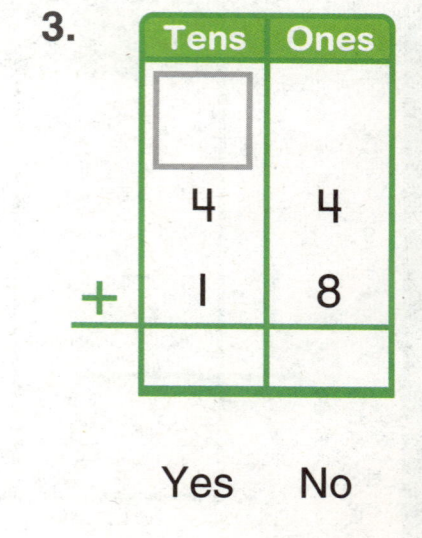

1.
Tens	Ones
1	
2	9
+ 2	3
5	2

(Yes)   No

2.
Tens	Ones
3	7
+ 2	2

Yes   No

3.
Tens	Ones
4	4
+ 1	8

Yes   No

Name _____

Independent Practice — Add. Use connecting cubes and your workmat.

4. | Tens | Ones |
|---|---|
| | |
| 2 | 7 |
| +5 | 5 |
| | |

5. | Tens | Ones |
|---|---|
| | |
| 1 | 9 |
| +3 | 2 |
| | |

6. | Tens | Ones |
|---|---|
| | |
| 4 | 3 |
| +1 | 7 |
| | |

7. | Tens | Ones |
|---|---|
| | |
| 1 | 4 |
| +2 | 1 |
| | |

8. | Tens | Ones |
|---|---|
| | |
| 3 | 1 |
| +4 | 9 |
| | |

9. | Tens | Ones |
|---|---|
| | |
| 5 | 6 |
| +3 | 3 |
| | |

10. | Tens | Ones |
|---|---|
| | |
| 5 | 7 |
| +1 | 5 |
| | |

11. | Tens | Ones |
|---|---|
| | |
| 6 | 5 |
| +1 | 6 |
| | |

12. | Tens | Ones |
|---|---|
| | |
| 3 | 9 |
| +1 | 8 |
| | |

13. | Tens | Ones |
|---|---|
| | |
| 1 | 2 |
| +5 | 6 |
| | |

14. **Higher Order Thinking** Draw the second addend.

First Addend   Second Addend   Sum

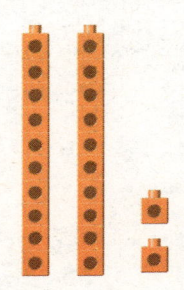

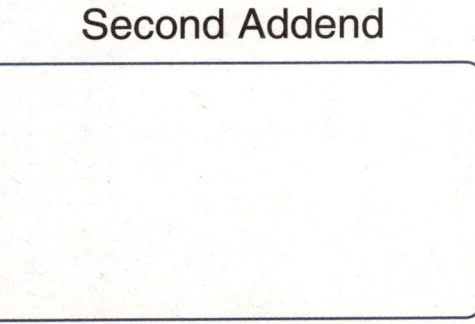

Step Up | Lesson 4

eight hundred sixty-five 865

Problem Solving
Solve the problems below.

15. **Use Tools** Trent builds a fort with 28 blocks. Ryan uses 26 blocks to make it bigger. How many blocks are used in all?

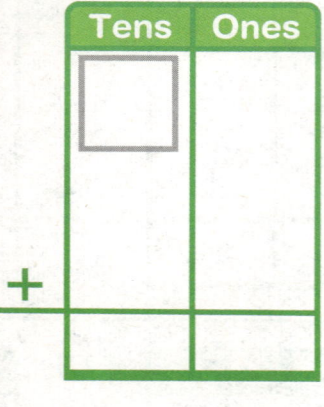

Tens	Ones
+	

_____ blocks

16. **Use Tools** Greg counts 32 buttons. Then he counts 30 more. How many buttons does Greg count in all?

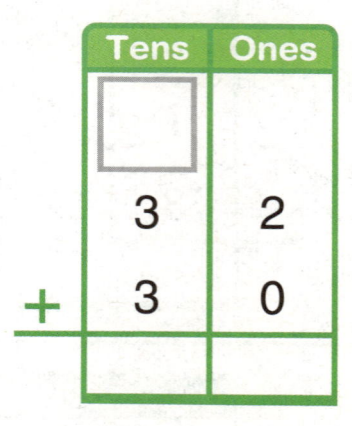

Tens	Ones
3	2
+ 3	0

_____ buttons

17. **Higher Order Thinking** Write an addition story about the notebooks and pencils in your classroom. Use pictures, numbers, or words.

18. **Assessment** Maria has 33 pennies. Her mom gives her 19 pennies and 7 nickels. How many pennies does Maria have now?

Ⓐ 41
Ⓑ 49
Ⓒ 51
Ⓓ 52

Name _____

Step Up to Grade 2

Lesson 5
Subtract on a Hundred Chart

Solve & Share

How can you use the hundred chart to help you solve 57 − 23? Explain. Write a subtraction equation.

1	2	3	4	5	6	7	8	9	10
11	12	13	14	15	16	17	18	19	20
21	22	23	24	25	26	27	28	29	30
31	32	33	34	35	36	37	38	39	40
41	42	43	44	45	46	47	48	49	50
51	52	53	54	55	56	57	58	59	60
61	62	63	64	65	66	67	68	69	70
71	72	73	74	75	76	77	78	79	80
81	82	83	84	85	86	87	88	89	90
91	92	93	94	95	96	97	98	99	100

I can …
subtract two-digit numbers from two-digit numbers using a hundred chart.

I can also model with math.

____ − ____ = ____

Step Up | Lesson 5

eight hundred sixty-seven 867

Find 43 − 28 using a hundred chart.

I need to find the **difference** between 28 and 43.

Start at 28. Count to the next number that matches the ones in 43.

21	22	23	24	25	26	27	28	29	30
31	32	33	34	35	36	37	38	39	40
41	42	43	44	45	46	47	48	49	50

Count by ones! I counted 5 ones to get from 28 to 33.

Count by tens to 43.

21	22	23	24	25	26	27	28	29	30
31	32	33	34	35	36	37	38	39	40
41	42	43	44	45	46	47	48	49	50

That's 1 ten, or 10 more.

I added 5 and 10. That makes 15.

28 + 15 = 43
So, 43 − 28 = 15.

Do You Understand?

Show Me! How can you use a hundred chart to find the difference between 18 and 60?

☆ Guided Practice ☆

Subtract using the hundred chart. Draw arrows if you need to.

21	22	23	24	25	26	27	28	29	30
31	32	33	34	35	36	37	38	39	40
41	42	43	44	45	46	47	48	49	50
51	52	53	54	55	56	57	58	59	60
61	62	63	64	65	66	67	68	69	70

1. 58 − 24 = 34

2. 41 − 21 = _____

3. _____ = 53 − 32

4. 64 − 23 = _____

868 eight hundred sixty-eight

Step Up | Lesson 5

Name _____

Independent Practice
Subtract using the hundred chart. Draw arrows if you need to.

1	2	3	4	5	6	7	8	9	10
11	12	13	14	15	16	17	18	19	20
21	22	23	24	25	26	27	28	29	30
31	32	33	34	35	36	37	38	39	40
41	42	43	44	45	46	47	48	49	50
51	52	53	54	55	56	57	58	59	60
61	62	63	64	65	66	67	68	69	70
71	72	73	74	75	76	77	78	79	80
81	82	83	84	85	86	87	88	89	90
91	92	93	94	95	96	97	98	99	100

5. 86 − 34 = _____

6. _____ = 77 − 42

7. 55 − 22 = _____

8. 88 − 51 = _____

9. 73 − 21 = _____

10. _____ = 98 − 56

11. 82 − 61 = _____

12. **Higher Order Thinking** Write the digit that makes each equation true.

57 − ☐2 = 15

7☐ − 36 = 42

48 − ☐1 = 17

98 − 37 = ☐1

56 − ☐2 = 34

89 − ☐3 = 26

Step Up | Lesson 5

eight hundred sixty-nine 869

Problem Solving

Use the chart to solve each problem below.

13. Enrico's puzzle has 75 pieces. Enrico fits 53 pieces together. How many more pieces does Enrico still need to fit together to complete the puzzle?

_____ − _____ = _____

_____ pieces

41	42	43	44	45	46	47	48	49	50
51	52	53	54	55	56	57	58	59	60
61	62	63	64	65	66	67	68	69	70
71	72	73	74	75	76	77	78	79	80
81	82	83	84	85	86	87	88	89	90
91	92	93	94	95	96	97	98	99	100

14. Reasoning A book has 65 pages. Gloria needs to read 22 more pages to finish the book. How many pages has Gloria read already? _____

15. Higher Order Thinking Felix wants to subtract 89 − 47. Write the steps Felix can take to subtract 47 from 89 on the hundred chart.

16. ✓Assessment Lee has 98 marbles. 23 of the marbles are blue. 14 marbles are green. The rest of the marbles are red. How many marbles are red?

Ⓐ 37
Ⓑ 61
Ⓒ 75
Ⓓ 84

Name _____

Solve & Share

There are 22 students drawing pictures. 4 of them finish drawing. How many students are still drawing? Use cubes to help you solve. Show the tens and ones you have.

Tens	Ones

_____ tens   _____ ones

22 − 4 = _____

Step Up to Grade 2

Lesson 6
Models to Subtract 2- and 1-Digit Numbers

I can ...
use a model to subtract a 1-digit number from a 2-digit number.

I can also use math tools correctly.

Step Up | Lesson 6

Digital Resources at SavvasRealize.com

eight hundred seventy-one 871

Find 32 − 5.

There are not enough ones to subtract.

Tens	Ones
|||	::

−
Tens	Ones
3	5

Regroup 1 ten as 10 ones.

Write 2 to show 2 tens. Write 12 to show 12 ones.

−
Tens	Ones
2 3	12 5

Subtract the ones. Then subtract the tens.

−
Tens	Ones
2 3	12 5
2	7

There are 2 tens and 7 ones left.

So, 32 − 5 = 27.

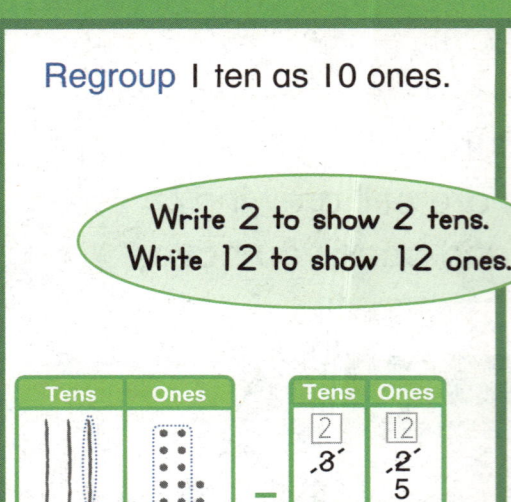

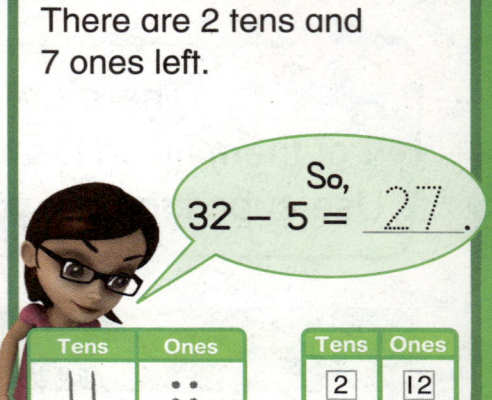

−
Tens	Ones
2 3	12 5
2	7

Do You Understand?

Show Me! Why do you need to regroup when you subtract 32 − 5?

☆ **Guided Practice** ☆ Subtract. Draw place-value blocks to show your work. Regroup if you need to.

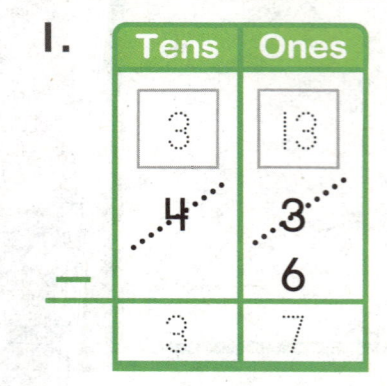

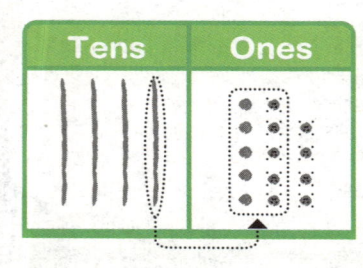

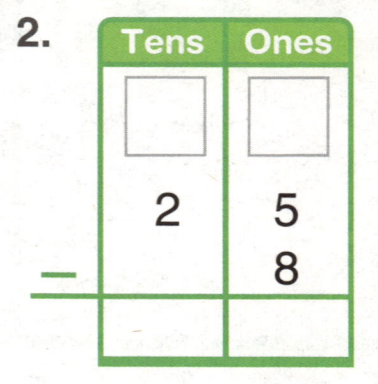

1.
Tens	Ones
3	13
4	3
	6
3	7

Tens	Ones

2.
Tens	Ones
2	5
	8

Tens	Ones

872 eight hundred seventy-two

Step Up | Lesson 6

Independent Practice

Subtract. Draw place-value blocks to show your work. Regroup if you need to.

3.
Tens	Ones
☐	☐
3	3
	3

Tens	Ones

4.
Tens	Ones
☐	☐
9	1
	4

Tens	Ones

5.
Tens	Ones
☐	☐
6	1
	9

Tens	Ones

Write the missing number in the box.

6. **Higher Order Thinking** What numbers will complete the subtraction equations?

☐ − 9 = 17   43 − ☐ = 37

Step Up | Lesson 6

eight hundred seventy-three 873

Problem Solving Solve the problems below.

7. Reasoning There are 14 students playing with blocks. 9 students go home. How many students are still playing with blocks?

Tens | Ones

_____ students

8. Reasoning There are 13 books on the shelf. Amy takes 2 of them. How many books are left on the shelf?

Tens | Ones

_____ books

9. Higher Order Thinking What mistake did Monica make when she subtracted 24 − 4? Show how to fix her mistake.

```
  24
-  4
  10
```

Tens | Ones

10. Assessment Liesel collected 36 leaves. She put some of them in a book. She had 9 leaves left. How many leaves did she put in the book?

Ⓐ 27
Ⓑ 37
Ⓒ 28
Ⓓ 45

Name _____

Solve & Share

An airplane is due to arrive at 3:15.
How can you show this time on the clock below? Explain.

Step Up to Grade 2

Lesson 7
Tell Time to Five Minutes

I can ...
tell time to the nearest 5 minutes.

I can also look for things that repeat.

Step Up | Lesson 7

eight hundred seventy-five   **875**

Both clocks show 8:05.

minute hand

The minute hand moves from number to number in 5 minutes.

To tell time to five minutes, count by 5s. Both clocks show 8:35.

I can start at 8:00 and count by 5s to tell the time.

There are 60 minutes in 1 hour.

hour hand

The minutes start over again each hour.

Do You Understand?

Show Me! The time is 9:35. What time will it be in 5 minutes?

In 15 minutes?

In 25 minutes?

Guided Practice

Complete the clocks so both clocks show the same time.

1.  4:15

2. 2:35

3. :

4. 1:25

876 eight hundred seventy-six

Step Up | Lesson 7

Name _____

Independent Practice Complete the clocks so both clocks show the same time.

5.

6. 7:10

7.

8. 12:25

9.

10.

11. **Number Sense** Complete the pattern.

9:20   9:15   9:10   :

Step Up | Lesson 7

eight hundred seventy-seven 877

Problem Solving Solve each problem.

12. Generalize What time is 15 minutes past the time on the green clock and 15 minutes before the time on the orange clock?

13. Number Sense Look at the time on the first clock.
What time was it 5 minutes ago? Write that time on the second clock.

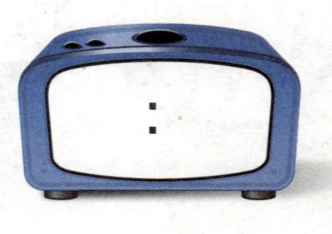

14. Higher Order Thinking Draw a clock that shows the time you wake up in the morning. Explain how you know you showed the correct time.

15. Assessment The minute hand is pointing to the 10. Which number will it be pointing to 10 minutes later?

Ⓐ 12
Ⓑ 11
Ⓒ 10
Ⓓ 9

Name _____

Solve & Share

What is another way to show 100? Draw a picture and explain.

Step Up to Grade 2

Lesson 8
Understand Hundreds

I can ...
understand place value and count by hundreds to 1,000.

I can also model with math.

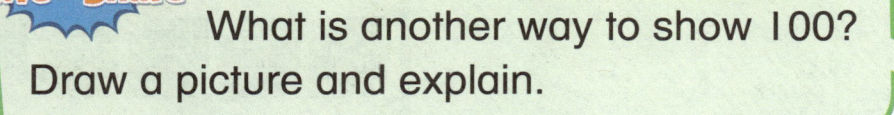

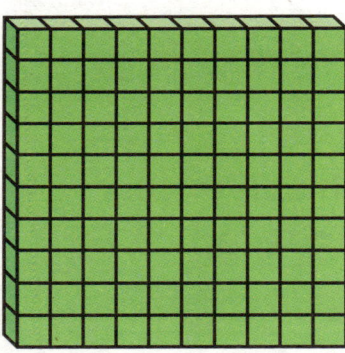

Way 1

Way 2

Step Up | Lesson 8   eight hundred seventy-nine 879

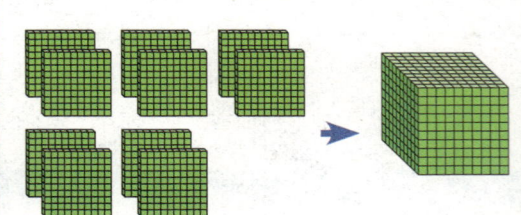

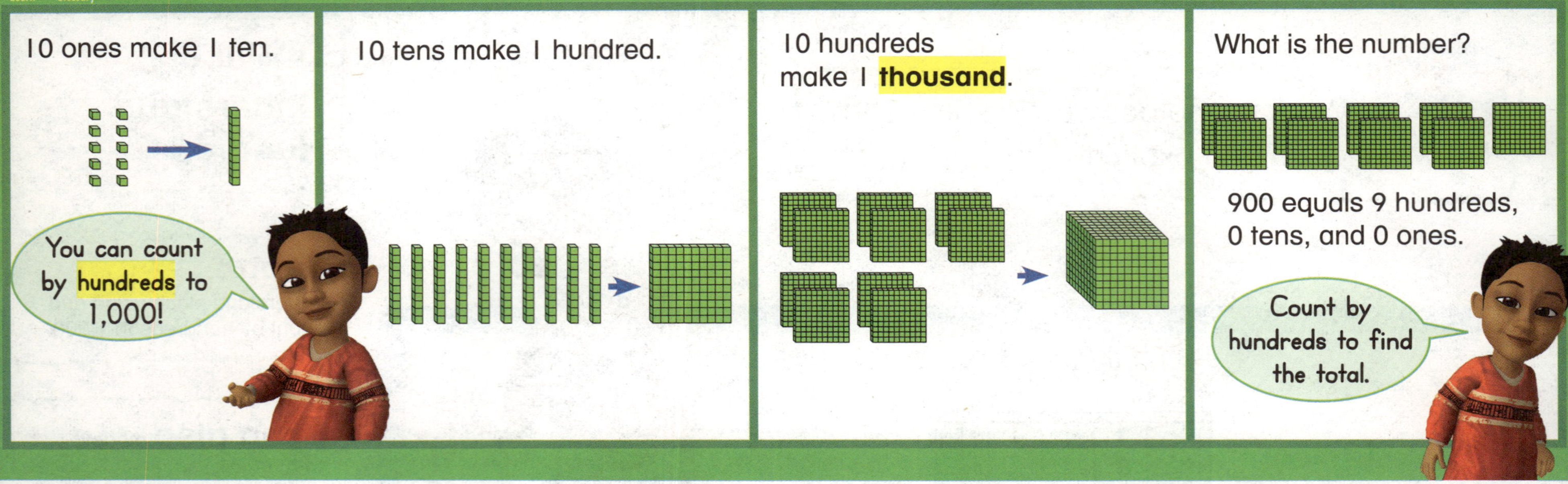

10 ones make 1 ten.

10 tens make 1 hundred.

10 hundreds make 1 **thousand**.

What is the number?

900 equals 9 hundreds, 0 tens, and 0 ones.

You can count by **hundreds** to 1,000!

Count by hundreds to find the total.

Do You Understand?

Show Me! 10 ones make 1 ten. 10 tens make 1 hundred. 10 hundreds make 1 thousand. Do you see a pattern? Explain.

Guided Practice

Complete each sentence. Use models if needed.

1.  _300_ equals _3_ hundreds, _0_ tens, and _0_ ones.

2. 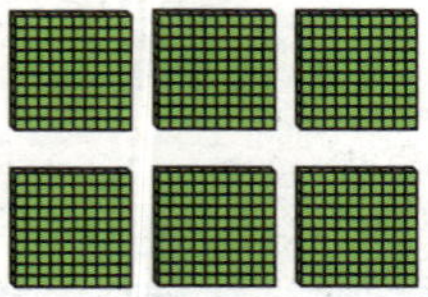 _____ equals _____ hundreds, _____ tens, and _____ ones.

880 eight hundred eighty

Step Up | Lesson 8

Name _____

Independent Practice
Complete each sentence. Use models if needed.

3. _____ equals _____ hundreds, _____ tens, and _____ ones.

4. _____ equals _____ hundreds, _____ tens, and _____ ones.

5. _____ equals _____ hundreds, _____ tens, and _____ ones.

6. _____ equals _____ hundreds, _____ tens, and _____ ones.

7. **Number Sense** Complete the pattern.

| 1,000 | 900 | 800 | | 600 | | 400 | 300 | 200 | |

Step Up | Lesson 8

eight hundred eighty-one 881

Problem Solving

Solve each problem. Use models if needed.

8. **Use Tools** Patti picked a number. She says her number has 2 hundreds, 0 tens, and 0 ones.

   What is Patti's number?

   _____

9. **Vocabulary** Complete the sentences using the words below.

   hundred   tens   ones

   There are 10 _____ in one hundred.

   There are 100 _____ in one _____.

Higher Order Thinking Pearl and Charlie are playing beanbag toss. Circle the two numbers they each must get to score 1,000.

10. Pearl has 200 points.

    200   500   600   100

11. Charlie has 700 points.

    100   200   400   700

12. **Assessment** Each box has 100 pencils. Count by hundreds to find the total. Which number tells how many pencils are in the boxes?

    Ⓐ 700
    Ⓑ 550
    Ⓒ 500
    Ⓓ 150

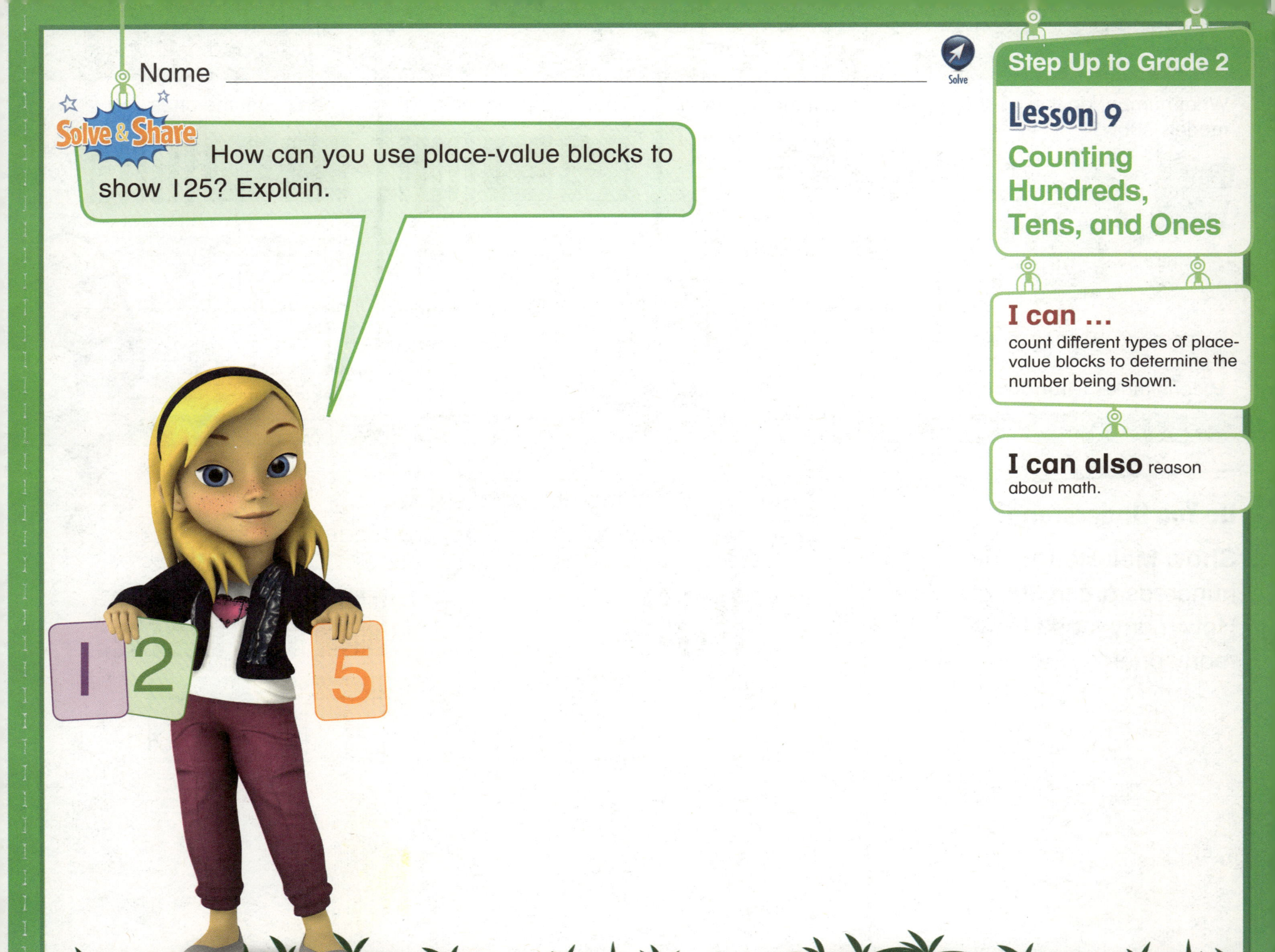

Name _____

Solve & Share

How can you use place-value blocks to show 125? Explain.

Step Up to Grade 2

Lesson 9
Counting Hundreds, Tens, and Ones

I can ...
count different types of place-value blocks to determine the number being shown.

I can also reason about math.

Step Up | Lesson 9

eight hundred eighty-three 883

What number do the models show?

Remember, 10 ones make 1 ten.
10 tens make 1 **hundred**.

First, count the hundreds.

Hundreds	Tens	Ones
2		

Then count the tens.

Hundreds	Tens	Ones
2	5	

Then count the ones.

Hundreds	Tens	Ones
2	5	9

The models show 259. 259 has 3 **digits**.

Do You Understand?

Show Me! How many hundreds are in 395? How many tens? How many ones?

Guided Practice

Write the numbers shown. Use models and your workmat if needed.

1.

Hundreds	Tens	Ones
	7	7

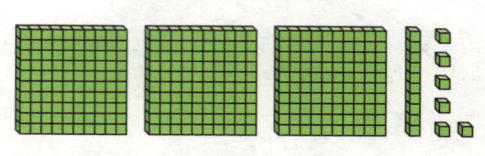

77

2.

Hundreds	Tens	Ones

Name _____

Independent Practice
Write the numbers shown. Use models and your workmat if needed.

3.

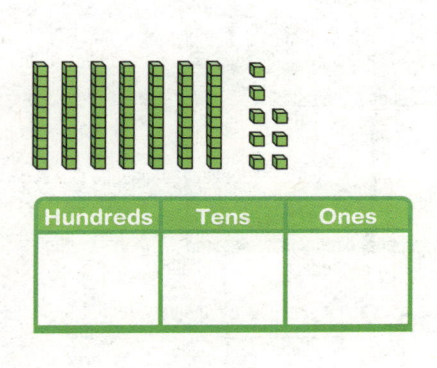

Hundreds	Tens	Ones

_____

4.

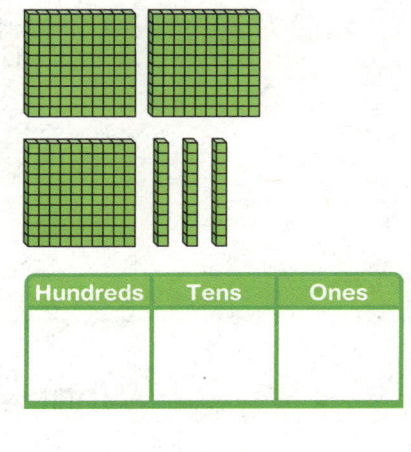

Hundreds	Tens	Ones

_____

5.

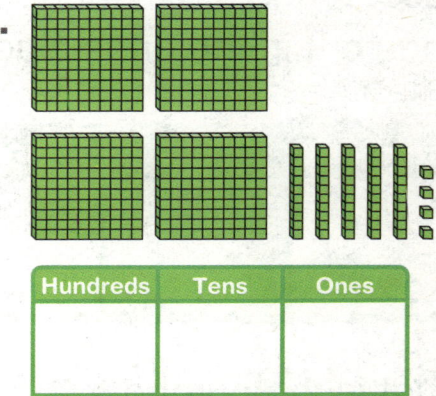

Hundreds	Tens	Ones

_____

6.

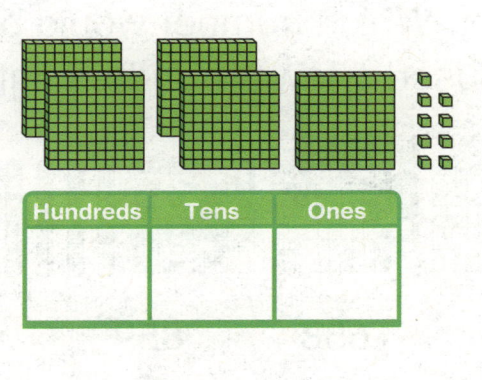

Hundreds	Tens	Ones

_____

7.

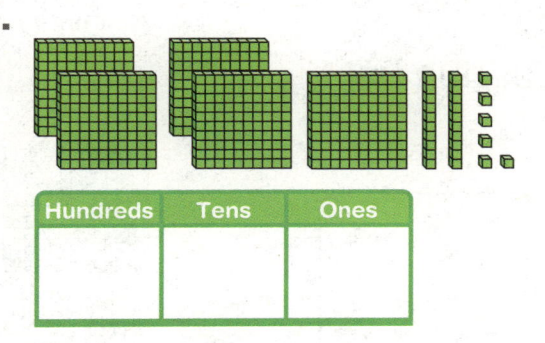

Hundreds	Tens	Ones

_____

8.

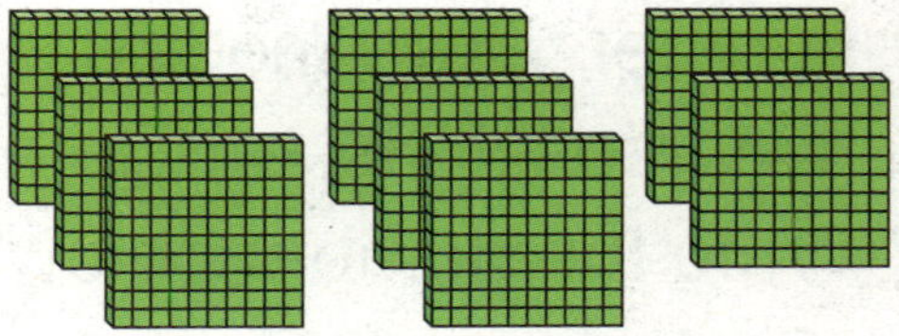

Hundreds	Tens	Ones

_____

9. **Higher Order Thinking** Find the number. It has 4 hundreds. The digit in the tens place is between 2 and 4. The number of ones is 2 less than 6. _____

Step Up | Lesson 9

eight hundred eighty-five **885**

Problem Solving Solve each problem below.

10. **Look for Patterns** Complete the chart. A number has a 6 in the hundreds place. It has a 0 in the tens place. It has a 4 in the ones place.

Hundreds	Tens	Ones

What is the number? _____

11. **Look for Patterns** Complete the chart. A number has a 4 in the hundreds place. It has a 7 in the tens place. It has a 0 in the ones place.

Hundreds	Tens	Ones

What is the number? _____

12. **Higher Order Thinking** Choose a 3-digit number. Draw models to show the hundreds, tens, and ones for your number. Write the number below.

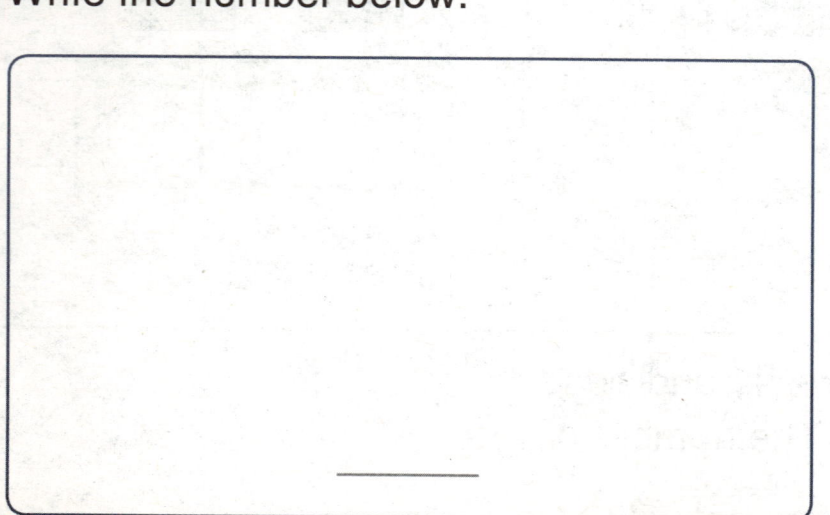

13. **Assessment** Max used these models to show a number. Which number would be shown if Max used 1 fewer hundred flat?

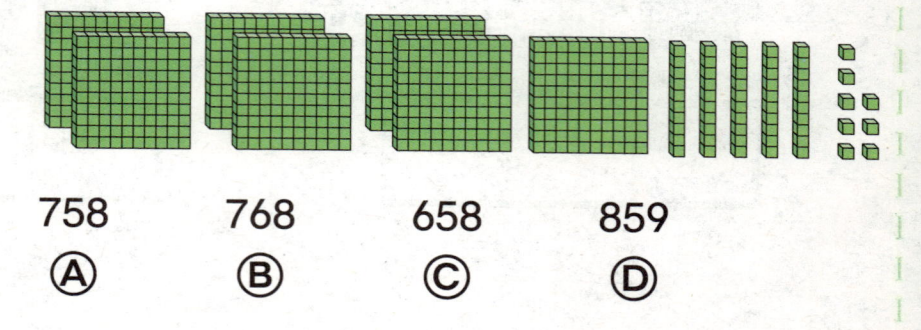

758   768   658   859
Ⓐ   Ⓑ   Ⓒ   Ⓓ

886 eight hundred eighty-six   Step Up | Lesson 9

Name _____

Solve & Share

Use the number line to skip count by 5s, starting at 0. Write the two missing numbers. Describe any patterns you see.

Step Up to Grade 2

Lesson 10
Skip Count by 5, 10, and 100, to 1,000

I can ...
skip count by 5, 10, and 100 using a number line.

I can also look for patterns.

0   5   10   15   20   ☐   ☐

_____
_____
_____

Step Up | Lesson 10 · eight hundred eighty-seven · **887**

This number line shows skip counting by 5s.

I see a pattern in the ones digits!

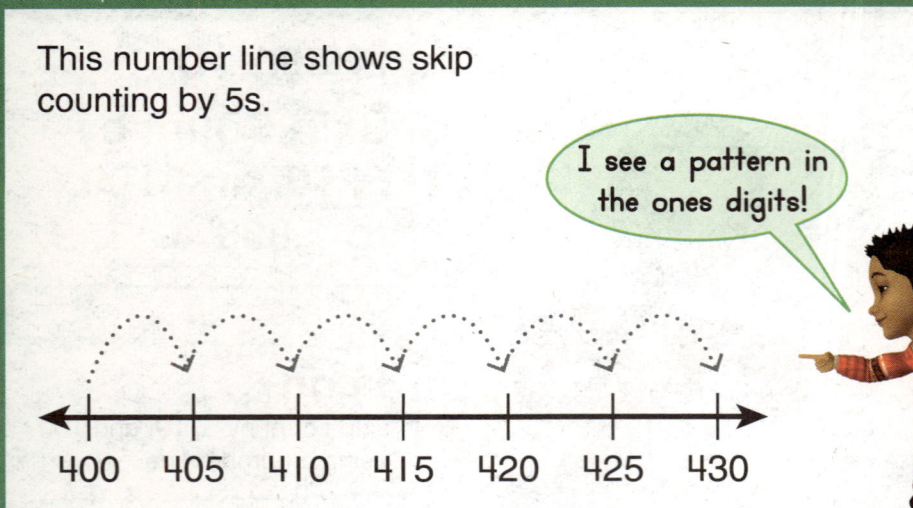

400 405 410 415 420 425 430

This number line shows skip counting by 100s.

I see a pattern in the hundreds digits!

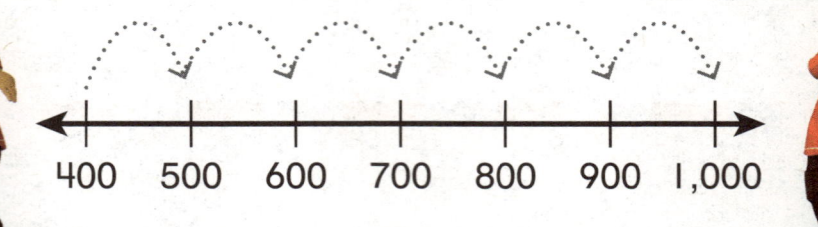

400 500 600 700 800 900 1,000

Do You Understand?

Show Me! How could you use the number line in the first box above to skip count by 10s starting at 400?

Guided Practice

Skip count on the number line. Write the missing numbers.

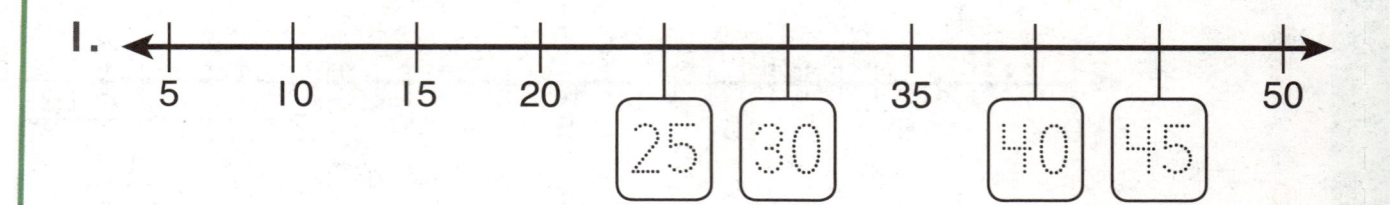

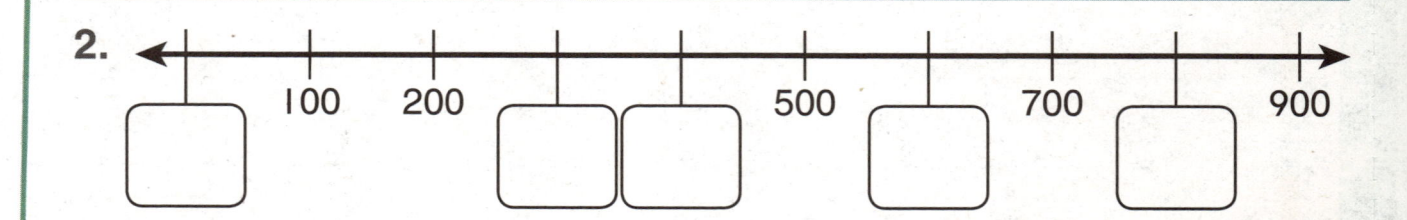

1. 5 10 15 20 25 30 35 40 45 50

2. 100 200 ___ ___ 500 ___ 700 ___ 900

888 eight hundred eighty-eight

Step Up | Lesson 10

Name _____

Independent Practice
Skip count on the number line. Write the missing numbers.

3. 10, [20], 30, 40, [50], 60, 70, [80], 90, 100, [110], 120, 130

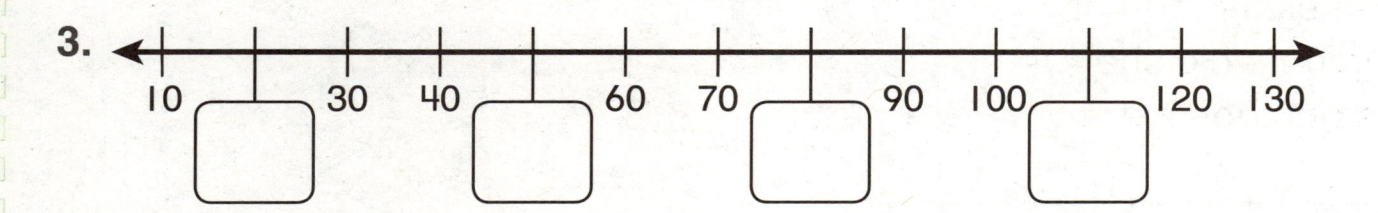

4. 400, 405, 410, [415], [420], 425, [430], [435]

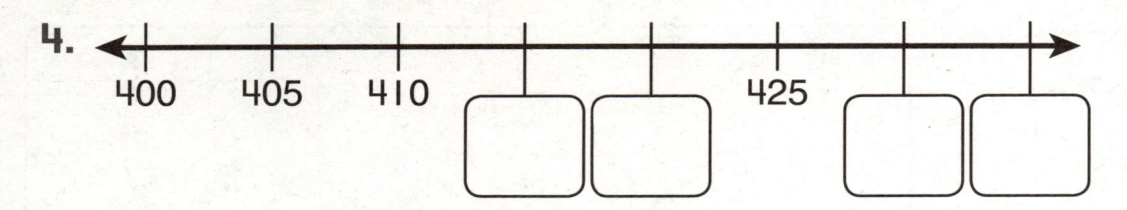

5. 520, 530, 540, [550], [560], [570], [580], 590, [600]

What's the pattern?

Step Up | Lesson 10

eight hundred eighty-nine 889

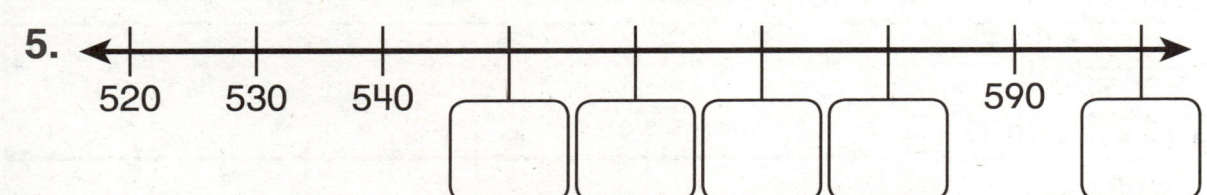

Problem Solving Skip count on the number line. Write the missing numbers.

6. **Look for Patterns** Jill completed part of the number line. What numbers did she leave out? Complete Jill's number line.

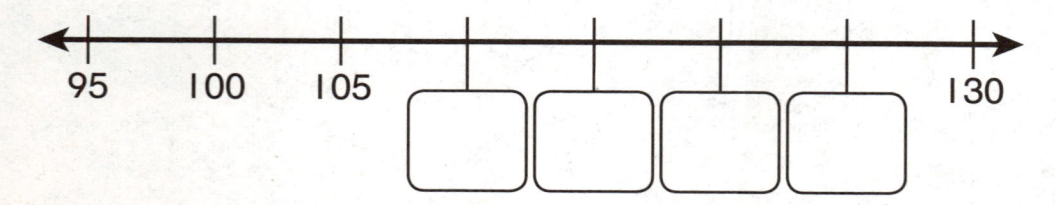

95 100 105 ☐ ☐ ☐ ☐ 130

7. **Higher Order Thinking** What number is used to skip count on this number line? How do you know?

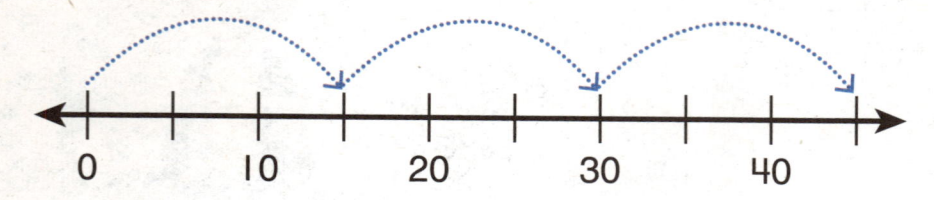

0 10 20 30 40

8. **Assessment** In his last four basketball games, Roy scored 10, 15, 20, and 25 points. By what number do Roy's points skip count?

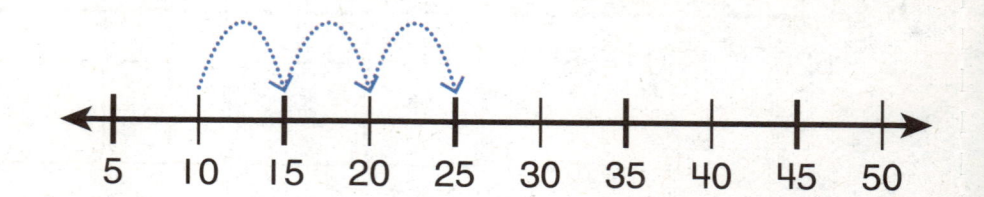

5 10 15 20 25 30 35 40 45 50

4 Ⓐ   5 Ⓑ   10 Ⓒ   25 Ⓓ

890 eight hundred ninety   Step Up | Lesson 10

Glossary

1 less

4 is 1 less than 5.

1 more

5 is 1 more than 4.

10 less

20 is 10 less than 30.

10 more

10 more than a number has 1 more ten or 10 more ones.

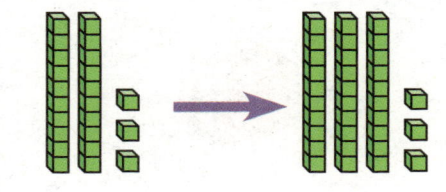

A

add

When you add, you find out how many there are in all.

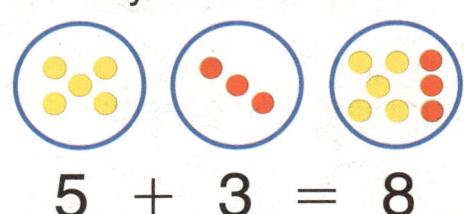

5 + 3 = 8

addend

the numbers you add together to find the whole

2 + 3 = 5

addition equation

3 + 4 = 7

addition fact

9 + 8 = 17

Glossary

G1

C

column

1	2	3	4	5
11	12	13	14	15
21	22	23	24	25
31	32	33	34	35

↑ column

compare

to find out how things are alike or different

cone

corner

count on

You can count on by 1s or 10s.

15, 16, 17, 18

20, 30, 40, 50

cube

cylinder

D

data

information you collect

Favorite Pets
cat
dog
cat
cat
dog

difference

the amount that is left after you subtract

$4 - 1 = 3$

The difference is 3.

digits

Numbers have 1 or more digits.

43 has 2 digits.
The tens digit is 4.
The ones digit is 3.

43

doubles fact

an addition fact with the same addends

$4 + 4 = 8$
↑ ↑

4 and 4 is a double.

doubles-plus-1 fact

The addends are 1 apart.

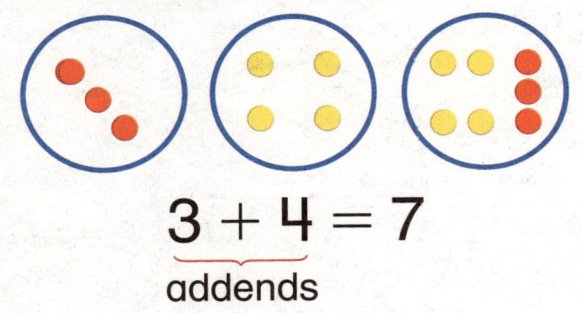

$$3 + 4 = 7$$
addends

doubles-plus-2 fact

The addends are 2 apart.

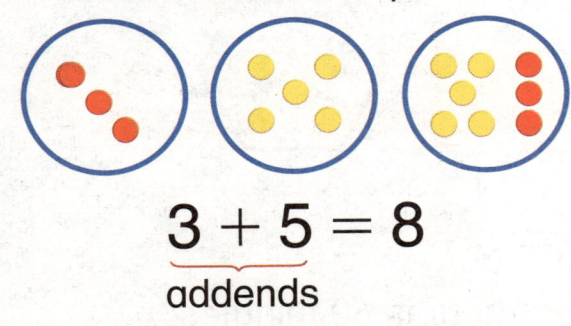

$$3 + 5 = 8$$
addends

E

edges

equal shares

4 equal parts

equal sign (=)

$$2 + 3 = 5$$
↑
equal sign

equals

5 + 2 equals 7.

equation

$6 + 4 = 10$ $6 - 2 = 4$

$10 = 6 + 4$ $4 = 6 - 2$

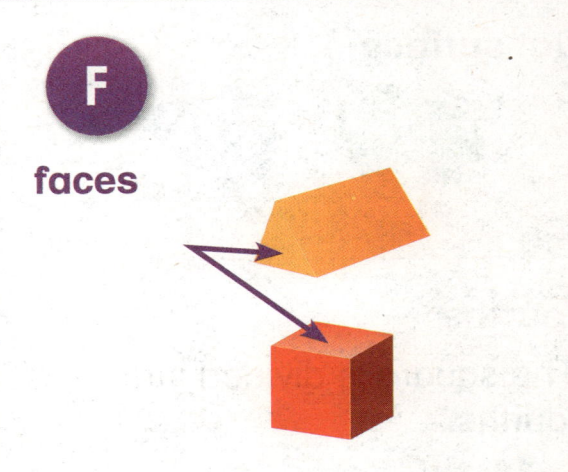

F

faces

fact family

a group of related addition and subtraction facts

$3 + 5 = 8$
$5 + 3 = 8$
$8 - 3 = 5$
$8 - 5 = 3$

fewer

A group that has less than another group

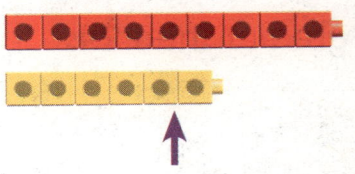

The yellow row has fewer.

Glossary

G3

flat surface

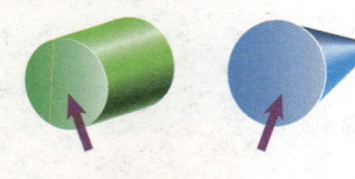

fourths
The square is divided into fourths.

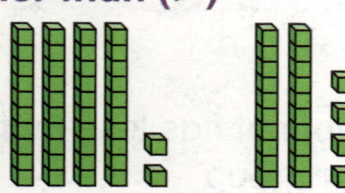

greater than (>)
42 is greater than 24.

greatest
the number or group with the largest value

7 11 23

23 is the greatest number.

H

half hour
A half hour is 30 minutes.

1:30

halves
The circle is divided into halves.

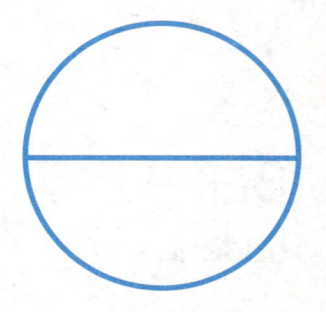

hexagon

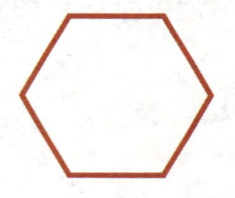

hour
An hour is 60 minutes.

2:00

hour hand

The short hand on a clock is the hour hand.
The hour hand tells the hour.

It is 3:00.

hundred chart

A hundred chart shows all of the numbers from 1 to 100.

1	2	3	4	5	6	7	8	9	10
11	12	13	14	15	16	17	18	19	20
21	22	23	24	25	26	27	28	29	30
31	32	33	34	35	36	37	38	39	40
41	42	43	44	45	46	47	48	49	50
51	52	53	54	55	56	57	58	59	60
61	62	63	64	65	66	67	68	69	70
71	72	73	74	75	76	77	78	79	80
81	82	83	84	85	86	87	88	89	90
91	92	93	94	95	96	97	98	99	100

I

in all

There are 4 birds in all.

inside

The dogs are inside the dog house.

J

join

to put together

3 and 3 is 6 in all.

L

least

the number or group with the smallest value

| 7 | 11 | 23 |

7 is the least number.

length

the distance from one end of an object to the other end

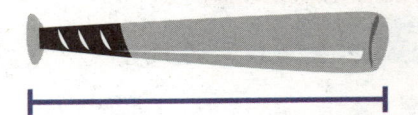

less

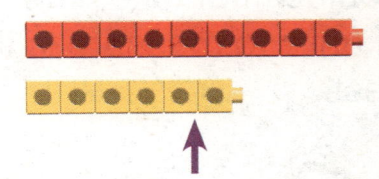

The yellow row has less.

Glossary

G5

less than (<)

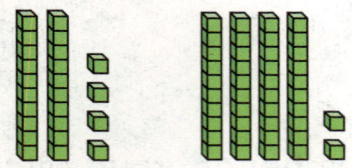

24 is less than 42.

longer

An object that is 7 cubes long is longer than an object that is 2 cubes long.

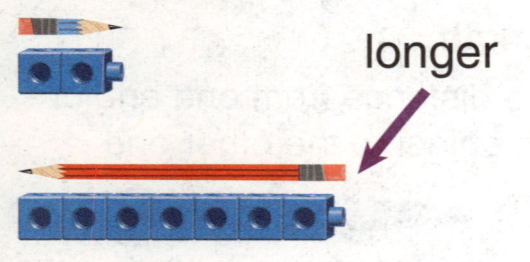

longer

longest

The object that takes the most units to measure is the longest.

longest

M

make 10

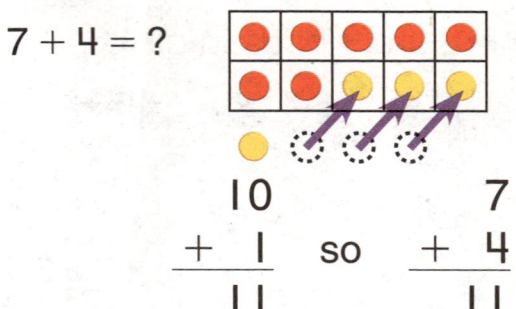

7 + 4 = ?

$$\begin{array}{cc} 10 & 7 \\ +\ 1 & +\ 4 \\ \hline 11 & 11 \end{array}$$

so

measure

You can measure the length of the shoe.

minus

5 − 3

5 minus 3

This means 3 is taken away from 5.

minus sign (−)

7 − 4 = 3

minute

60 minutes is 1 hour.

minute hand

The long hand on a clock is the minute hand. The minute hand tells the minutes.

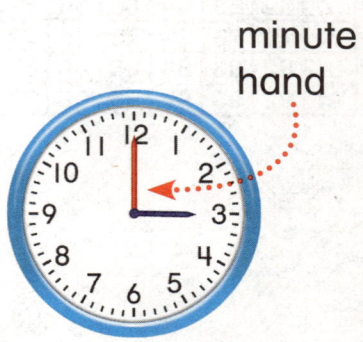

minute hand

It is 3:00.

G6　Copyright © Savvas Learning Company LLC. All Rights Reserved.　Glossary

missing part

the part that is not known

2 is the missing part.

more

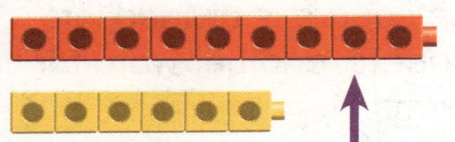

The red row has more.

N

near double

an addition fact that has an addend that is 1 or 2 more than the other addend

$4 + 5 = 9$

$4 + 4 = 8$. 8 and 1 more is 9.

number chart

A number chart can show numbers past 100.

81	82	83	84	85	86	87	88	89	90
91	92	93	94	95	96	97	98	99	100
101	102	103	104	105	106	107	108	109	110
111	112	113	114	115	116	117	118	119	120

number line

A number line is a line that shows numbers in order from left to right.

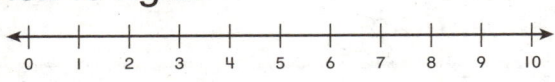

O

o'clock

8:00
8 o'clock

ones

The ones digit shows how many ones are in a number.

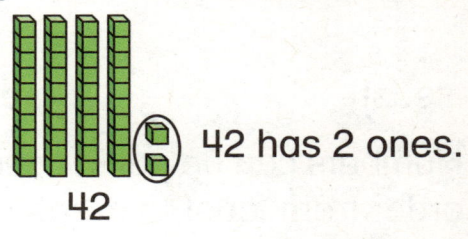

42 has 2 ones.

42

ones digit

The ones digit in 43 is 3.

43

ones digit

open number line

An open number line is a number line without marks in place.

Glossary

G7

order

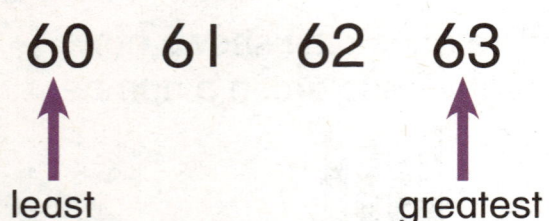

60 61 62 63

least greatest

Numbers can be put in counting order from least to greatest or from greatest to least.

outside

5 dogs are playing outside of the dog house.

P

part

a piece of a whole

2 and 3 are parts of 5.

pattern

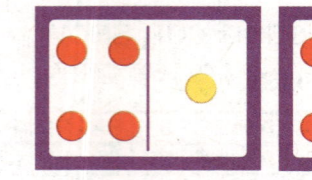

You can arrange 5 objects in any pattern, and there will still be 5 objects.

picture graph

a graph that uses pictures to show data

Favorite Pets			
Cat			
Dog			

plus

5 + 4

5 plus 4

This means 4 is added to 5.

plus sign (+)

6 + 2 = 8

Q

quarters

The square is divided into quarters, another word for fourths.

R

rectangle

G8 Glossary

rectangular prism

related facts
addition facts and subtraction facts that have the same numbers

$2 + 3 = 5$

$5 - 2 = 3$

These facts are related.

row

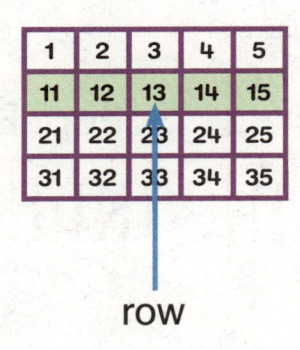

row

S

scale
A scale is used to measure how much things weigh.

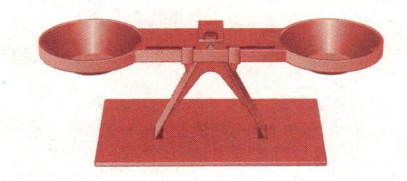

shorter
An object that is 2 cubes long is shorter than one that is 7 cubes long.

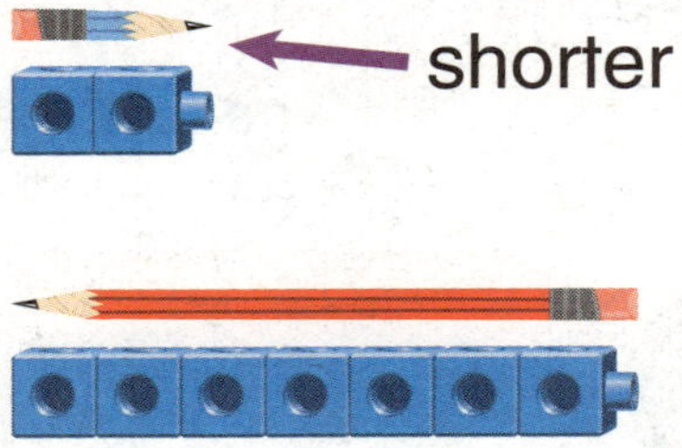

shorter

shortest
The shortest object is the one that takes the fewest units to measure.

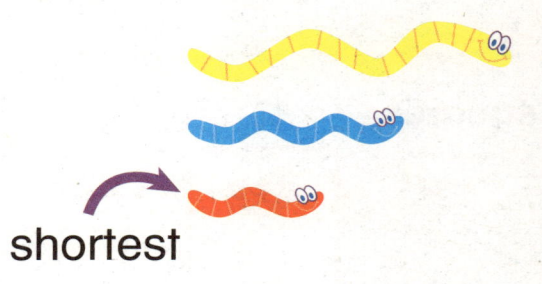

shortest

side
These shapes have straight sides.

sort
to group objects according to how they are similar

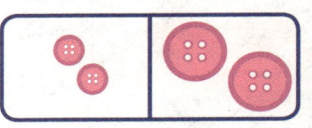

The buttons are sorted by size.

Glossary

G9

sphere

square

standard form

a number shown in digits

28

subtract

When you subtract, you find out how many are left.

$5 - 3 = 2$

subtraction equation

$12 - 4 = 8$

sum

$2 + 3 = 5$
↑
sum

survey

to gather information

Do you like cats or dogs better?

Cats |||
Dogs ||

T

take away

Start With	Take Away	Have Left
6	3	3

$6 - 3 = 3$

To take away is to remove or subtract.

tally chart

a chart that uses marks to show data

Walk	School Bus
𝍷𝍷𝍷𝍷𝍷 ||	𝍷𝍷𝍷𝍷𝍷 𝍷𝍷𝍷𝍷𝍷

Glossary

tally marks

marks that are used to record data

| Cats | ||||| |
| Dogs | || |

There are 5 cats and 2 dogs.

tens digit

The tens digit shows how many groups of 10 are in a number.

35 has 3 tens.

35

Three-dimensional (3-D) shapes

These are all 3-D shapes.

trapezoid

triangle

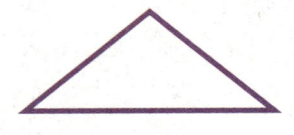

Two-dimensional (2-D) shapes

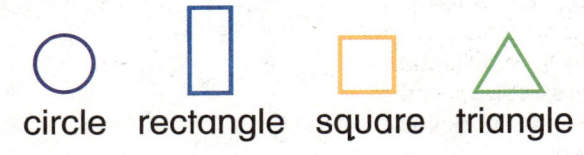

circle   rectangle   square   triangle

V

vertex (vertices)

a point where 3 or more edges meet

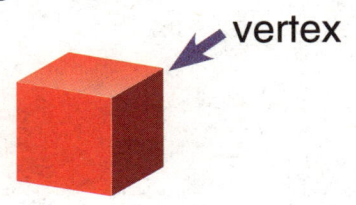

← vertex

W

whole

You add parts to find the whole.

5

The whole is 5.

Glossary

G11

enVisionmath 2.0

Photographs

Photo locators denoted as follows: Top (T), Center (C), Bottom (B), Left (L), Right (R), Background (Bkgd)

001 MattiaATH/Shutterstock;**075** Karen Faljyan/Shutterstock;**151L** fotografie4you/Shutterstock;**151R** Chris Sargent/Shutterstock;**227L** Galyna Andrushko/Shutterstock;**227R** Alexey Stiop/Shutterstock;**297** Willyam Bradberry/Shutterstock;**349C** Umberto Shtanzman/Shutterstock;**349L** Nick barounis/Fotolia;**349R** Gudellaphoto/Fotolia;**391** John Foxx Collection/Imagestate;**445L** Chaoss/Fotolia;**445R** Lipsett Photography Group/Shutterstock;**493** Anton Petrus/Shutterstock;**541L** Baldas1950/Shutterstock;**541R** Shooarts/Shutterstock;**609** Barbara Helgason/Fotolia;**661** Studio 37/Shutterstock;**705** Vereshchagin Dmitry/Shuhtterstock;**741** Sergey Dzyuba/Shutterstock;**813BL** Isuaneye/Fotolia;**813BR** Ftfoxfoto/Fotolia;**813TL** Sumire8/Fotolia;**813TR** Janifest/Fotolia.